STARTING FROM
GLASGOW

for Tony,
Joanna, Andrew and Tory

STARTING FROM GLASGOW

ROSEMARY TROLLOPE

FOREWORD BY

JOANNA TROLLOPE

SUTTON PUBLISHING

First published in 1998 by
Sutton Publishing Limited · Phoenix Mill
Thrupp · Stroud · Gloucestershire · GL5 2BU

Reprinted 1998

British Library Cataloguing in Publication Data
A catalogue record for this book is available from the British Library

ISBN 0 7509 1784 9

Cover picture: *The morning room at 2 Clairmont Gardens* by Rosemary Trollope.

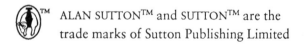

Typeset in 10/14 pt Sabon.
Typesetting and origination by
Sutton Publishing Limited.
Printed in Great Britain by
Ebenezer Baylis, Worcester.

Contents

Joanna, aged seven, and Andrew, aged two.

Foreword

This book started with a little memory of my mother's, called 'The White Shoes' (you'll find it on page 39). It was the summer of 1995, and Ian and I were staying with friends in Scotland. My mother wrote to me there. This was not unusual; my mother writes to me *every*where. In fact, I sometimes think, were I to cross the Gobi Desert, I should soon see a runner approaching across the vasty wastes bearing a trade mark long blue envelope in a cleft stick . . . But this particular letter contained something else, something my mother had written on impulse, years before, about her Glasgow childhood. I read it, re-read it, read it aloud to everyone in that Perthshire house, and then sent it off to the literary editor of the, then, *Glasgow Herald*.

He loved it. He passed it on to his features editor, Jackie McGlone, and she loved it. She loved it even more when she discovered that my mother could provide her own illustrations, too. The one article grew to many, and the many grew to be the substantial basis for a book – this book, written, illustrated, and even jacketed by my mother.

To call it a book of memoirs is misleading. It certainly is packed with memories of a vivid and fascinating childhood – a childhood so vivid, in fact, that it often seemed to my brother and sister and me to be more real than our own – but it is also a book of revelations, of what that childhood led to and how it shaped my mother's subsequent life and ideas and appetites.

It also – and this emerges strongly from the book – demonstrates how subtle and powerful those characterful, cultivated, comfortable Glasgow beginnings were. The secret of their strength lay in the fact that in some curious way my mother's childhood and my grandmother's childhood overlapped and interwove – the same house in Clairmont Gardens, the same secure nursery floor presided over by the same beloved nanny, the same domestic ritual. As my mother says herself, 'In my mother's nursery, time had stood still, so that her childhood joined ours without a break'. This was both an advantage and a disadvantage. It made for a wonderfully rooted base from which to set out into the world beyond, but it could also make that world seem a cold, painful, threadbare place by comparison.

Neither my mother nor my grandmother ever had any illusions about this. 'I sometimes think,' my grandmother once said to me, 'that a childhood like mine was no preparation for life at all.' My mother sensed this very early – read 'Miss Maguire' to see her adolescent appreciation of the emotional bleakness that could lie beyond the warmth of the nursery fire, or 'Tubbins' for a picture of the misery of sibling rivalry in even the best regulated of families. A robust dose of Scottish blood in them both ensured they understood clearly the pitfalls of privilege, yet those early years in the Glasgow cradle left them with the uncomfortable knowledge that nothing in life would be quite as interesting, or as wonderfully certain, ever again.

Yet those years also left my mother with much more. Her strong visual sense, her appetite for humanity and human oddity, her art, her pleasure in children and animals, her keen appreciation of atmosphere, all owe something at least to the varied and confident influences of her childhood. And, indeed, to Glasgow itself, a city still remarkable for its personality and its warmth – a very good city, in fact, from which to start.

Joanna Trollope

Tory, aged five.

Acknowledgements

Some of the contents of this collection have already appeared in the *Herald*, and I am much indebted to Jackie McGlone for her help and encouragement, and for accepting the first one before she knew I was in any way connected with Joanna.

Inordinately proud though I am to be Joanna's mother, and grateful for her generous professional help, it was a happy surprise (and surprise is the operative word because Joanna had sent it to the *Herald* in my name, unbeknown to me) to find myself unwittingly in print and Jackie McGlone asking for more.

I would also like to thank Julie Hodson and Sue Corfield for making recognizable ms out of my tangled sheets of A4 and for working against the clock on my behalf with such good grace.

Rosemary Trollope

J.D.H.

In 1926, my eighty-year-old Glasgow grandfather, James David Hedderwick, lay dying in his high-ceilinged, hushed bedroom in Clairmont Gardens. Everything in the room, as in all the house, was of the highest quality, and any sound of passing traffic was kept out by efficient double glazing which, like electricity and good central heating, he had installed on his marriage to my grandmother in the 1880s.

On the nursery floor above, my brothers and sister and I had to remember to keep quiet – not easy when I, at seven, was the eldest – and creep downstairs on tiptoe past his door if we were going out, so as not to disturb him.

He lay, silent and comatose, as he had been for the past two days, in the finest linen, under a quilt of deep blue shot silk (thoughtfully backed with black sateen so that it wouldn't slip off the bed), and on the sofa at the end of his bed lay his now unused Jaeger dressing jacket. It was the colour of a teddy bear and as soft as a cloud which I well knew, it being a favourite treat to sit on his bed, enclosed by a Jaeger-clad arm, while he read me *They Stole Little Bridget* or *The Fighting Temeraire* or *Young Lochinvar*, or to play dominoes on his bedside table.

Now his life was ebbing away and the eminent, knighted specialist was coming to see him. Peering over the nursery banisters, I watched the small rotund man, a huge gold watchchain on his spherical front clearly visible from above, being escorted upstairs by the maid.

'I know my way, Nessie,' he said testily. 'Good heavens, I know my way here.' Nessie affected not to hear and sailed on ahead of him. As she knew very well, deferential as my grandmother was to all doctors and especially to this one, for the medical knight to appear in the bedroom unannounced was unthinkable.

So it was that, after examining the almost lifeless patient, the doctor sat down to write out a prescription. He took his gold fountain pen from his pocket with a flourish. Fountain pens were at that time still a very smart item to own. My grandmother adored them, and her loving and indulgent husband had already given her three, a tortoiseshell one, a silver, and a gold. Being him, he had first done his market research and all three pens functioned perfectly. (The manufacturer would have had some questions to answer if they had not.)

Grandad should also have chosen the doctor's pen, which failed utterly to write. The little man shook it irritably and tried again, in vain. Shaking it violently a second time, he was interrupted by a deep voice from the bed. 'Away home, you dirty wee brute, and shake that pen over your own Persian carpet,' said my grandfather. What a mercy it was that my grandmother, appalled and delighted in equal parts, was present to record this for family posterity.

My grandfather has received many honours for a lifetime of public work. He had been a JP and LLD and also Lord Dean of Guild Court twice over. As such he was Glasgow's second citizen after the Lord Provost. Treasuring this honour as he did, he must have looked on with delight from the celestial spheres when his grandson, Richard Hedderwick Barclay, became Lord Dean exactly thirty years later (by special concession since the Dean of Guild Court had by then ceased to exist, and he was a lawyer).

His most lasting work was probably as a member of the Board of Management of the Royal Infirmary when they installed electricity in the hospital in 1887. I don't know his part in that vital decision, but he was a man of vision. How could he, from his house with perfectly running electricity, when most of his neighbours – and all the hospitals – were content with gas, not have pushed for electricity?

It was to be seven years before he began his long stint as Chairman of the Board, to preside over the rebuilding in honour of Queen Victoria's Diamond Jubilee. The *Glasgow Herald* wrote 'No man who had not high aims, great confidence in his fellow men, and resistless courage would have dared to face the sea of cares which beset the Chairman of the Managers at this time.'

The rebuilding was, however, triumphantly completed, and in June 1914 the King and Queen came to open the 'vast new hospital, so equipped as to be in the very forefront of medical and surgical science'. As indeed it was, and already had worldwide fame for its radiology department among other successes.

In Bavaria, in 1895, Professor Wilhelm Conrad von Röntgen had discovered X-rays. Only a matter of weeks later, because it had electricity and because 'there were lively minds at work in this age of enlightenment', the Royal opened the world's first hospital X-ray department in January 1896, and it is still one of the best. Not that I would know about that, but a very distinguished radiologist (from the Western, so he must have been telling the truth) gave me these interesting facts.

All I know is that Grandad loved the Royal ardently, and even picked out his burial plot in the necropolis so that his Celtic cross would face the hospital. Whenever I have thought that perhaps a necropolis is not the most encouraging view from hospital windows, I have remembered that nothing could be better for any patient than the lurking spirit of my warm-hearted, clever, and enthusiastic grandparent.

Though dignified and exemplary in public life he was far from alarming at home, and often mischief led him into situations which delighted children and disconcerted his wife. She was sweet-natured, dutiful, formal, and anxious, with only a very small sense of humour, and much younger than he was (his first wife having died in childbirth leaving two little daughters whom we knew as beloved aunts). Above all things she wanted to please him and this was a happy situation since he was not hard to please and he loved her dearly and was very proud of her when she sang and played the guitar at dinner and house parties. Later, he was proudest of all when she was awarded the OBE for her charity work and he felt this was an achievement beyond anything he had done.

It was early in their marriage, however, when they decided one day to meet at the plumber's showroom and choose all the fittings for a new bathroom. He, concerned in every detail of life, took a keen interest in all things domestic, and she wouldn't have dreamed of choosing cushions or curtains, or china or glass without him. (Any more than he would have thought of consulting any but his own palate when it came to restocking his excellent cellar.)

I don't know which of the bathrooms was to be redone. Not for him the contemporary paucity of nineteenth-century bathrooms: there were five in his house, including one on the maids' floor, and also an alarmingly well-thought-out 'gents' on the ground floor, where children were only taken in moments of crisis.

As my grandmother pattered down the street towards the shop, she saw him standing waiting for her and broke into a run. 'Don't run, dearie,' he shouted, but she took no notice and scuttled on hampered by high heels, long swirling skirts and an elaborate, pinned-on, Edwardian hat. So he cupped his hands around his mouth and let out such an almighty roar that everyone in the street was brought to a standstill. Heads shot out of cab windows, cabbies screwed round in alarm and pedestrians, frozen in their tracks, recovered mobility and came running back to see what was happening and what all the noise was about. Surely it couldn't have emanated from the stately bearded gentleman escorting his pink-faced little wife into the shop?

My grandmother's trials were not over. Once inside, he took off his highly polished shoes and climbed into various baths, lying down to see how comfortable they were and if the taps and soap dishes were well placed. He tried out washbasins, pretending to wash his hands and lose the soap to see how easy it was to retrieve it. Then, to her despair, he sat on several of the lavatories, not in the least caring that these were in the shop window. She hid at the back of the shop, praying that none of their friends would be among the laughing passers-by.

One of his great charms for children was that he regarded them as sentient beings and a vital part of the human race, and so he treated them accordingly, always careful of their dignity. When my six-year-old mother was taken to a service in the Baptist church and found it a lively change from the long, long services at Park Church, where her father was an elder, she came home much inspired and asked her father if she might join the Temperance Society. He considered her question carefully, and then said, 'Well dearie, that is indeed an undertaking. But I tell you what. If you can keep off the whisky until you are ten, then I will pay your subscription.' She accepted this

J.D.H.'s cutter *Annasona*, winner of many prizes including the Queen's Cup at Cowes.

proposal as seriously as it was given, and only when retelling it in adult years, would collapse in laughter.

He was also an excellent sailor. His yachting days were over before I was born, but the dining-room sideboard was laden with magnificent gold and silver trophies won by his remarkable 40-foot cutter, the *Annasona*.

Stories from the yachting days abounded, however, and indeed of the yachting parties. (I still have the yachting 'silver'. The silver plating is worn very thin, but the J.D.H. on each spoon and fork is clear. There is a great deal of it, eighteen of everything. Some yacht: some parties . . .)

On one voyage round the Hebrides Grandad went ashore at a small village to top up supplies. He found a little grocer's shop and set about the lengthy business of buying what he needed. Butter and cheese to be cut from big slabs, biscuits and tea to be measured out from deep drawers, flour from a sack on the floor. All these had to be done up in little packets and the idea was to enclose them all in a parcel tied with string. My deft, neat-fingered grandfather watched in growing dismay as the grocer fumbled with this task, and tea fell on the butter, and flour fell all over the counter, and finally he said, 'Here, let me do it'. The grocer was happy to stand back and see what he could do, and was soon filled with admiration at the final neat, tidy parcel, firmly knotted and with a string loop to carry it by.

'Man,' he said, beaming. 'That's grand. Really *grand*. I can see you are in the trade.'

This compliment gave Grandad great and lasting pleasure which endured all his life. Sometimes he delighted us, his grandchildren, by writing us tiny letters in tiny envelopes, or giving us a miniature parcel containing something like a silver threepenny bit or a jujube, and if I said, 'How could you make it so wee?' he would say, 'Because I am in the trade,' and laugh all over again at the memory of the admiring Highland grocer.

In the summer, my grandparents did as many of their friends and relations did, and rented a country house for several months. This great migration involved considerable generalship, but both grandparents were expert. The country house would be filled with family and friends from near and far, and my grandmother would order her daily supplies from all her usual Glasgow shops and these would be delivered by train.

All the Glasgow-based men commuted daily to their offices and practices by the same means. In order to make it all feel home-like, cushions and lamps and everything off the morning-room writing table, as well as linen and favourite pillows and a case of books, was also transported. My mother remembered a room where eight or ten huge, domed 'ball dress' trunks stood open, ready to be filled for the summer holiday.

One year, when I was four, and my younger brothers three and one, Grandad rented Kelburn from his friend, the then Lord Glasgow. This was magnificent, as there was plenty of room for all and sundry. Not only aunts and uncles and cousins and friends, but remote figures who came because they had alway been there, on the fringe of the family, even if few people could then remember why. A lady with grey hair and a moustache called 'Batty', and an awkward young woman called 'Pegs', and various elderly men in thick flannel trousers and blazers and panama hats of whom we children were as wary as they were of us.

It was decreed in those days that all small children had a morning rest. (I would hate to try that idea on a four-year-old today; we must have been very docile.) My rest at Kelburn was delightful, in a hammock slung between the trees, and as a bonus Grandad came every morning and swung the hammock with his walking stick crook, and gave me a rich tea biscuit and a chat before pottering off again.

Three-year-old David, harnessed into one of our two big brown prams, became jealous and who could wonder? So it was arranged that the next day we would swap, and he would rest in the hammock, and I in the pram. Whenever I am asked if I can remember being in a pram I can say with most agonized memories that I can. Who wouldn't, stuffed into a pram at four? The length of my legs has always been a problem, right up to the time when some decent

hosiery manufacturer thought of making extra-long tights, and stuffed into the pram, with my legs concertina-ed and no way of moving them, I was in torture. I couldn't even sit up because I was prudently strapped in. (Fidgety children had been known to overturn even this huge heavy pram, and my younger brother soon became adept: I can clearly remember him bellowing from under the upturned pram on the Kelburn lawn.)

I lay examining the key-pattern moquette braid – cream on brown – inside the hood, and even as I think of it can smell again the rubbery smell of the hood in the hot sun. My rescuer, however, was seeking me. Failing to find me in the hammock, Grandad's welcome figure suddenly loomed up between me and the sun. 'Childie, what on earth are you doing there, all crumpled up?' he said, and when I explained he said briskly, 'Well, we're not having any more of that. I never heard such nonsense', and unbuckled the straps and held the pram while I climbed out. 'What about my rest?' I asked. 'You'll live without it' he said. 'Come away into the summer house with me and we'll read'.

It was bad luck on David, and a fine example of life not being fair, especially as he too could read and we much enjoyed reading together, but I was too relieved to be out of the pram to think of anything else. Grandad, however, was nothing if not fair. Every second day after that David had the hammock and I rested on my bed indoors, where Grandad always visited me for a chat before he went out on his wander in the garden.

He left, when he died, four daughters and a son, and many grandchildren and now of course great-grandchildren and great-great-grandchildren. So I do hope some of his marvellous qualities have filtered down through the generations. His standards, of honour and rectitude and compassion and integrity, were high: it would be nice to think we were living up to them, but he was unique. Sometimes, however, one of us gets it right. I was in the middle of writing this when the telephone rang and we received the joyful news that his great-granddaughter, our eldest child, had been awarded the OBE, 'for services to literature'.

That, I know, would have given him immense pleasure.

In-laws

My Scottish mother met my English father on a cruise to Norway, so it was a welcome bond when it transpired that her grandparents and his parents lived only a few miles from each other in Gloucestershire.

Not that they were friends. They never could be. His mother, Mrs Hodson, the wife of the charismatic and rather theatrical Rector of Oddington, bustled about her teeming, untidy rectory, fortified by her satisfaction in her distinguished pedigree, and despising Lady Apperly – who sat, stately and formal, in her huge luxurious house, Rodborough Court – because Sir Alfred Apperly was in trade. Lady Apperly certainly knew of Mrs Hodson, but her scorn – for being plain and careless of her appearance and having a baby every year for nearly ten years so that she was now surrounded by an inconceivable number of unruly boys and one indulged, pretty, tearful daughter – easily outdid any compassion she might have felt for their contrasting circumstances. We could never understand why Grandma Hodson took such pride in her antecedents, as we could only judge by the horrible old great-uncles she wheeled out as examples. One particularly repellent great-uncle came to stay with us for what seemed weeks and weeks, and my brothers and sister and I spent ages trying to calculate how *little* Maskew blood ran in our veins, a discussion usually finalized by the youngest of us saying firmly 'Well, I'm the smallest so I've got the least'.

The Apperlys, had they cared, could have produced a decent enough pedigree, going back to Stephen de Apperly, who had received a general pardon from Edward III for his good service in 'the war of France' but there was no doubt about the trade. Alfred had inherited a wool mill from his father which made fine, prize-winning cloth and which had won the Gold Medal at the Great Exhibition of 1851, and another for the finest cloth in all the world. After twenty-five Gold Medals, the firm received the 'Filestation Du Jury' at the Brussels Exhibition of 1910 and the same at Turin a year later. By this time, of course, Alfred had been in control of the firm for thirty years, and had added more mills, all in the Stroud Valley, and a model farm on which he grew his own excellent wool: he had become fed up with having to import it all from the Colonies, and the home wool trade was at that time in the doldrums. King Edward and Queen Alexandra were both so delighted with the beautiful 'Hydea' cloth which emanated from the aristocratic sheep at Hyde Farm that they ordered it thereafter by the bolt, and had endless suits made of it. Alfred was knighted for his services to the Liberal Party, and must have been a great help to them because he did nothing by halves.

He was an excellent, imaginative, employer, never happier than when updating his workers' housing, funding medical treatment, training his employees to use ever more modern machinery, and seeing that their children went to school well shod. He was exceedingly proud of his trade and his achievements, and would have been much surprised if he had picked up the derisory signals from Oddington Rectory.

He was a small bouncy little man with a neat pointed beard and a slightly simian look. Eager and active (in sharp contrast to his wife who simply sat all her life as far as I can tell, waited on by an army of servants and a devoted spinster sister-in-law known as 'Little Em') he would say after lunch each day 'Just twenty minutes, dear' and then would sit in an upright chair, one leg tucked under him like the Lincoln Imp, and sleep for exactly twenty minutes. He then shot off back to the mill, to solve a dozen problems, and make a score of plans, and have a whole lot of brilliant ideas and set them going. Energy and enthusiasm shone from him like the 'glory' round angels in Victorian pictures.

Which is just as well, because his wife possessed neither to a marked degree. Apart from a Sunday expedition to church there is only one other record of her rising from her chair. An aunt who had loved staying at Rodborough as a child, told of expeditions to Bath, 30 miles away, so that her grandmother could have a fitting at Jollys, and then there would be lunch at Fortes afterwards. A journey which would have seemed very long and tedious had she not been allowed to sit on the box, with Daniels, the coachman, who was her great friend.

This, I think, is the only record of Marie Apperly doing anything other than sitting. She died when I was seven, but to my eye this stately and formidable great-grandmother was at least 7 feet tall and dressed in stiff black brocade and lace and diamonds, her pearl-white hair undulating in symmetrical waves under a black velvet bow. In fact, I learned later to my con- siderable astonishment, she was barely 5 feet tall. What she actually did, or ever had done (bar producing three boys and three girls, all of whom were at once handed over to nurses and governesses and then boarding schools, including the girls, who went to the new and progressive Cheltenham Ladies College) was never clear. Except sit.

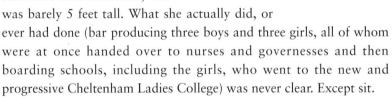

That I saw and can vouch for.

There was nothing the matter with her physically, and when, in her old age, she came to stay in her daughter's tall Glasgow house, I watched her glide easily up and down the long green-carpeted stairs between the armchair in her bedroom (covered in a grey and lavender and pink linen in a blurry design called jaspé) and the velvet-covered chair in the morning-room, where she took so long over the *Glasgow Herald* that her daughter ordered two copies for the duration of her visit. From this chair she only moved for meals (apart from one other glide up and downstairs to change for dinner), and her progress into the dining-room was so smooth she looked as if she rolled on casters. I can't remember ever seeing her smile, though I can easily recall her amiable expression of welcome, accompanied by 'Well, dee-*ur*', her rather deep voice dropping and lingering over the end of the word. After that a wise child kept out of her orbit. Her dark, hooded eyes seemed only there to seek out faults in speech, behaviour and posture. At the age of six, I was subjected to a long, bewildering treatise on how a young lady should behave, engendered, I discovered at long last, by my sin in being observed standing with my arms akimbo.

I can't imagine that this sedentary, passive lady provided much input when her husband, heartened by his expanding business and all the Gold Medals and international awards, decided to build himself a suitable house. He bought a sizeable house on Rodborough Hill, a couple of miles from Stroud, called The Hawthorns, and the farm next to it. He rebuilt The Hawthorns as the vast, lavish, exuberant Rodborough Court and the farm became Home Farm.

Rodborough Court – which I knew intimately by hearsay from my mother's detailed descriptions but never actually saw until it had become offices – was built exactly as he wanted and contained everything he admired. The result was enough to make the editor of the present-day interior decorating glossy curl up and shrivel away. An elaborate Elizabethan staircase descended into a Gothic hall decorated with a rich, three-dimensional brown and gold wallpaper. The doors were of elegant Regency proportions and the finger-plates and door handles complicated and handsome brass, the very latest in 1870s design. Everywhere there were cornices and corbels and carvings and ceiling-roses, from which descended showers of lights enclosed in silk shades with sparkling beaded edges.

All this, of course, before the stunned eye reached the furniture.

Although it was a fashion then to over-furnish, Rodborough Court must have been in a class of its own. Rumour, current among the irreverent younger members of the family in Glasgow, had it that Grandpa bought his pictures by size, asking his dealer to send him '3 six feet by four, two a bit smaller, and a dozen for the south-west bedroom'. Certainly the crimson silk wall-covering in the drawing-room hardly got a look in, so closely was the chaos of paintings hung there and moving about the room was quite hazardous, large as it was, considering the plethora of occasional tables, all laden with silver-framed photographs and ornaments and bibelots. The confidence behind the making of this house is, to our nervous contemporary eyes, amazing. Alfred and his ilk had no need or desire for professional advice when it came to decor. He engaged an architect, a nephew-by-marriage, Percy Horder, to build the house, and no doubt paid him *extremely* well – as was his wont: he was a most popular employer at all levels – because I have seen some elegant and discreet houses built by Horder as well as this pièce de résistance.

Ultimately, of course, the strong and undeviating taste of one man, however eclectic, has its own charm (*vide* the Burrell Museum!) and so it was with Rodborough Court, where grandchildren, with or without their parents, gathered in the summers and enjoyed it to the full.

The Rodborough summers were full of delights. The large indoor swimming pool, where the uncles entertained children by diving for pennies, the nearby Home Farm, trips with Grandpa in the gig to the mill or Hyde Farm, and riding on Rodborough Common in the care of Daniels the coachman, or if you were too small to ride, being conveyed there in wicker panniers strapped to the broad back of a staid pony for a picnic on the hillside. For the Glasgow family all this and the country joys such as playing barefoot on the grass, were a special treat.

As was their arrival, after the long, tedious train journey, and driving from Stroud station, up the drive, to see light streaming from the porch, and Grandpa and Aunt Em rushing out to meet them with hugs and kisses. Even in those days, Granny waited in the drawing-room ('well, my dee-*urs*') and she had to be greeted before they were able to rush excitedly to the familiar nurseries, and seek out the welcoming and equally familiar maids.

The head housemaid was called Rodman. Not because that was her name, but because long ago Granny had had a head housemaid called Rodman who had left to marry, and Granny appeared too idle to remember another name. So all the poor Violets and Mabels who entered the Apperly household as under housemaids, hoping to climb the career ladder and eventually become head housemaid, knew that if they did this they would have to become 'Rodman' in their turn. (I knew the last Rodman, a stern woman with much to be stern about, as by then she had to function as cook, housemaid, parlourmaid and all to the widowed Lady Apperly and her hired 'companion' in a spacious flat near Sloane Square. Rodborough Court and its contents and the whole wonderful lifestyle had been lost by the brother who succeeded Alfred, but had none of his brother's ability or judgement.)

Like all the grandchildren, my mother had the happiest memories of Rodborough Court and all the cousins, some nice, some awful, but all recalled for us, her children, in vivid detail. She was good at the risible aspect, even when applied to herself, and therefore told us exactly what happened when she heard that she had a little brother. She was two years and one month old, happily bare-foot as she picked daisies in the garden, and then became aware of two large grown-up feet standing by her, and far above her head an aunt said 'Do you know, dear, you have a baby brother? We have just heard from Glasgow. Isn't it lovely?' It was too, after five daughters, but that didn't strike the two-year-old. As she went on picking daisies she was thinking 'I will pick a *lot* of daisies and I will give them all to my baby brother and everyone will say "Oh Mollie darling what a *good kind* little girl you are to be thinking of your baby brother instead of yourself".' She probably guessed right. She was very much beloved and indulged, but what a sharp reminder that story is to anyone who might underestimate what can go on in a two-year-old head.

This moment in time, however, was all years before the day when the eldest Apperly daughter Ethel, aged twenty, small, pretty, efficient, and a talented player of both the organ and the Spanish guitar, to which she sang in her clear, boyish, well-trained voice, announced that she wanted to marry a Scotsman, James Hedderwick. Her parents must have been thrown. They had never met, and indeed had barely heard of him, Ethel having met him when she went to stay with a school friend in Glasgow. He was forty-five, had been a widower for thirteen years and had two adolescent daughters. He was an extremely successful stock-broker, assiduous in public and charitable work, an elder of the Church, and overwhelmingly in love with their little blonde daughter, as she was with him. It can't have been what they had had in mind for her, but she would clearly not be deflected so it was arranged that they would all meet in London, whence James often came on business, so that he could ask, formally, for her soft little hand.

They met at his hotel. They must have been an odd quartet. James looked fully his age, and Ethel much less than hers and though the two men were almost contemporaries and had much in common – both were extremely successful in their careers, both were clever and far-seeing, and both ardent in fulfilling their civic duties and responsibilities – they had far more in contrast. James also lived well, in a large and comfortable house, and like almost all Glaswegians, was aware and appreciative of the creative arts, so that in his house paintings were sought and bought with care, and the furnishings and colours throughout the house were subtle and harmonious and all of finest quality; he could never abide the shoddy or pretentious.

When he and Ethel embarked on married life they decided on every household detail together, and did so as long as he lived, and they were quite dashing by the standard of the day in the decor they chose. How about a peculiar Egyptian burnt-orange colour for the paint in the nursery? On all doors, the deep skirting boards and the long double-glazed windows, paint of such quality that it remained glossy and unchipped until the day in 1939 when the house was requisitioned by the Army. Quality, in point of fact, was the key to everything James owned. Nothing showy or opulent or ostentatious. Just the best that he could find.

From this warm, quiet house (the heavy doors all closed soundlessly on their well-oiled hinges) he set forth on his first visit to Rodborough and his wedding. Alfred met him at Stroud station, hurrying up the platform with loud cries of 'Welcome, Hedderwick! Welcome to Rodborough!', as James, in his exquisitely tailored suit, his Inverness cape piled on top of the excellent and much-used leather baggage on the porter's barrow, walked towards him.

If Rodborough Court was to be a shock to his discreet Scottish senses, it was nothing to the shock which awaited him in the station yard. There stood the Rodborough Court landau, festooned with garlands of flowers, with liveried postillion and outriders at the ready, all set for the hotly embarrassing drive through the streets of Stroud. The whole town knew Alfred, of course, so he enjoyed himself hugely, smiling and waving and doffing his Billycock hat, and calling out 'Here he is! Here he is!' to all and sundry. Everyone was aware of the impending wedding. The *Stroud News*, wishing the couple well, had mourned that they were about to lose 'The Rose of Rodborough and the Sunshine of Stroud'. She, like her father, was a popular figure. Later James, who became truly fond of his exuberant father-in-law, commented that it was lucky that his darling wife was worth the ordeal of that drive . . . His reaction to Rodborough Court can only be imagined, but at least it provided a splendid background for a splendid wedding with eight grown-up bridesmaids wearing huge, black, ostrich-feather-trimmed 'Gainsborough Lady' hats, and bearing tall slender black canes with bunches of flowers at the top.

The bride wore deep cream satin and priceless lace, and a wreath of beautiful French wax orange-blossom which had been worn by her mother. (In due course my mother wore it, and so did I, and so did my daughters and granddaughters and it is still in good enough shape for a great-granddaughter, if weddings by then still take place.) That evening there was a ball in the house, and the bride changed into yellow moiré, with heavy yellow net swagged and looped all over it. (We have the tiny bodice still and I doubt if in 1997 a six-year-old could get into it.)

Water lilies, containing night lights, floated on the swimming pool as guests drank champagne around it, and lights were planted all along the terraces, in the herbaceous borders, and in the bowers behind the classical statues, and under the huge *grandiflora magnolia* which climbed up one side of the house and around all the bedroom windows. It might not have been quite James's idea of a wedding reception but it presaged a long and very happy marriage so it must have been a good one.

When Alfred died in 1913, the *Stroud News* reported that 'there was a rare combination of qualities in Sir Alfred Apperly. The foresight, thoroughness, capacity in finance, daring courage and an immense energy, united with a kindliness of temper, and a genial humour that made him a charming friend. Few could tell an apt story as he could. Or throw a light and witty allusion into an argument.'

Given all that – and I am sure it had a lot of truth in it – it is all the more surprising that he chose such a dull, formal, and humourless wife. Or perhaps he knew exactly what he was doing, and that there was room in the house for only one personality as large and highly coloured as his own, and he needed, as balance, a predictable totem-person. Someone who could be relied upon to be permanently in the over-furnished drawing-room, beautifully dressed and contributing nothing positive.

'Well, my dee-*urs*. . . .'

Nuck

There are a few people – not many but a few – who, by the strength of their personality, affect the lives of those around them quite as much as a great inventor or famous leader or whatever, albeit from a modest base.

Nuck, my mother's Aberdonian nanny, was one. She acted more as a mother to my mother, whose own mother, although loving, was absorbed in being the perfect wife to a much older husband who, when they married, was already deeply absorbed in civic and charity work as well as his own demanding career, and she took to this life like a duck to water. In any case, 100 years ago, when my mother was born, it was normal in such a household to engage a nurse for the baby as soon as the monthly nurse, who cared for both mother and baby during the thirty days during which the mother had to retire to her post-natal bed (how did she *bear* it?) had departed.

So Nuck arrived at 2 Clairmont Gardens, Glasgow, aged twenty-six, the same age as her employer, and stayed there for the rest of her life. She was the daughter of a hard-pressed farmer, doubly hard-pressed because he had a family of twelve children, and the living to be made from the stony ground near Aberdeen, in the harsh climate, was meagre.

There were no photographs of Nuck's parents to supplement her stories – there wouldn't have been a single farthing to spare for anything so trivial. It would have been nice to be able to begin, visually, at the beginning, for of course by the time my brothers and sister and I were listening to all the riveting family tales and adventures the clan had spread to a vast network of nephews and nieces and great-nephews and great-nieces and even a baby or two added on to that.

We were told, however, that Nuck took after her father, and since she was tall and slender and upright as a plank to her dying day, it was easy to picture tall thin Mr Thomson standing by the breakfast table eating his porridge. He always stood, saying 'a standing sack fills best' but I dare say he had other motives as there were not enough chairs and benches for everyone to sit down, even with the small ones sitting with their porridge bowls on logs by the fire.

Only once a week, on Sunday, he sat down to breakfast, when he had his Sabbath boiled egg. Sometimes this was the only egg that Mrs Thomson had been able to keep back from the market, but she insisted that he should have it, as he worked so hard, and went without so much. All the same he couldn't bear to eat it all himself, so he sliced off the top, and each child in turn had the top of his egg for a treat.

It impressed me very much, hearing this, to think that each child therefore had to wait three months for his or her tiny treat. In spite of the weekly egg, poor Mr Thomson fell ill and died when Charles, the eldest, was only just into his twenties (Charles's name was pronounced 'Charrel' to rhyme with barrel, and never 'Chahss' in the careless English fashion. Aberdonians are rightly proud of the fact that they are often considered to be the true custodians of our language.)

Charles, having already been for years hard at work on the farm, walked 4 miles to Aberdeen University and 4 miles back as often as he could, in the evenings when the day's work was done. In due course he acquired a degree and also, inevitably, made many friends from different places and widened his horizons. He learned that farming in the soft South was a very different matter, and that the same amount of work would bring twice or thrice the reward, so he went down to Kent to see if the tales were true. They were. He returned, sold the farm for the pittance it was worth, stowed his mother and brothers and sisters and all the stock and indignant crated hens, and the cart and wagon and plough and harrow, and all the household goods, on to a ship and they sailed down to Chatham. The voyage took ages and though it was an adventure it was a tiring one, Nuck said, for the older children, with the stock to care for and young brothers constantly in danger of falling overboard, and at the end of it there was, of course, no soft home-coming. Charles had bought a derelict farm near Snodland, so on the quayside the horses had to be harnessed to the vehicles, and the vehicles laden with as much as possible, the rest being left to be fetched next day. Mrs Thomson and the youngest were installed on the wagon in a comfortable armchair fashioned from bags of oats and flour, and the next two youngest rode on the horses' backs, and all the others walked, driving the cows and sheep ahead of them. It must have been an exhausting walk, but no doubt, if Nuck was an example of the Thomson ethos and I am sure she was, they were sustained by the knowledge that they were in God's hands, and He would care for them.

So He did, with considerable help from Charles and all the children who were old enough to work on the farm. Mrs Thomson and her daughters, Jane (Nuck) and Catherine and Jessie, were fully occupied in cooking and baking and laundering and sewing and growing the vegetables – the latter being a new surprise and treat in the much more gentle climate. Mrs Thomson yearned for one of the newly invented sewing machines, but never had one. All the sheets and shirts and tablecloths and underwear were made by hand and all the jerseys and stockings and socks knitted by hand. (It was no wonder that Nuck's Singer sewing machine, in the Clairmont Gardens nursery, was the joy of her life.)

The locals in Kent were not welcoming, suspicious of strangers, and assuming that the large, respectable, but clearly impoverished family were barbarians. When the Thomson boys ploughed the fields using horses in tandem, men would gather behind the hedge to see such a strange sight, and shout derisively 'One man, one horse! Go you back where you came from with your heathen ways!' They were even more confused when Mrs Thomson, though clearly in need of every available hand to help with all that was to be done in restoring the farm to working order, no matter how youthful, turned up at the school to enrol all the eligible children. There, of course, they scored, Scottish education then being far ahead of English, and in any case the children were accustomed to working hard, and from the school-room a grudging respect for the immigrant family began to spread.

By the time the children were grown, and Catherine and Jessie married as did most of their brothers, they were all quite at home in

Kent, and many of them had nearby farms of their own of various kinds. One of them owned a fruit farm, and all through my childhood, in the cherry season, two huge dress-boxes full of cherries would arrive by post (the post was absolutely overnight and certain in those far-off days). One box would contain shiny, opulent black cherries, and the other white-hearts, like little beautiful apples with one creamy cheek and one rose-red. There must have been 12 lbs or so in each box, but we made short work of them, with due gratitude to Nuck's brother.

The next generation all became nurses and doctors and ministers and school teachers and missionaries, and legion though there were, we knew all their names and activities and characteristics. 'Tell us about Ian in India' we would plead 'Tell us about Isobel having to find that cottage in the snow to deliver the baby'.

Nuck always obliged, telling her stories in a factual and matter-of-fact way, never histrionic, always the bare truth and so very satisfying. Only one nephew let the side down and was seldom referred to, 'Poor Mary', Nuck would sigh, 'having a son like that'. He had become an actor. A perfectly respectable actor, working in reputable plays and theatres, and seldom out of a job, but all the same. . . . The rest of them were so exemplary that the phrase 'Nuck's Nephew' has passed into the language of our family. (As in 'What's the new fiancé like? Does Elisabeth approve of him?' and the reply would be 'Oh of course she does. He's sheer Nuck's nephew'.)

Once her mother was well supplied with daughters-in-law to help her, Nuck was free to pursue her chosen career, and took a job as nurserymaid in a large house in Eaton Square. Though she loved the children in her care she disliked London and the cold London ways, and having progressed through undernurse to nurse – which was what constituted nanny-training in those days – was delighted to find herself back in her beloved Scotland, in Clairmont Gardens. From here, for the rest of her life, letters in her neat angular hand issued forth by the ream to all her relations, so quite soon all of the Thomsons knew all about all of the Hedderwicks and vice versa. It meant, of course, that if ever one met a member of the other family there was instant familiarity and many dear friends.

The Hedderwick offspring – Bob, Gaickie, Nan, Mollie and Maynie.

Nuck must have been very attractive when young, so tall and slender, with her curly hair and bright eyes and her long neck. She remained, all her life, immensely distinguished in appearance. She was always very well dressed. A good tailor made her long narrow jackets and long narrow skirts, always dark grey or navy blue or black. Under these went silk blouses, one or two of them of wonderfully old-fashioned cut (since she was frugal, and the excellent silk was in good condition) with leg of mutton sleeves and rows of tiny covered buttons and pin-tucks all over the place. She *always* wore, with these blouses or dresses, or pullovers of fine quality, on all occasions, a lace insert at her throat, climbing up her neck with little bones at the sides to hold it up, which I think was a left-over from Edwardian days for ladies whose necks had become elderly and stringy. Her sharp wit and uncompromising views on right and wrong, made her seem rather alarming to various cousins, but for my brothers and sister and me she was so woven into our lives, all of us having been born in the house, and all our holidays and festivities and so on being spent in Nuck's nursery, that she was simply part of our lives, and a very essential and eternal part at that.

When she died, after a stroke in her eighties, I was with her. My mother, her adored Mollie, hastened from England but didn't arrive while Nuck was still conscious. It didn't matter, however, because Nuck, already a bit confused, thought that I, then a seventeen-year-old student at the Glasgow School of Art, was Mollie, who had been just that twenty-two years before. So, through me, Mollie was with her when her long, inspiring – for such integrity and such love is very inspiring – life ended, it seemed that she went forth in great content and confidence to meet her Maker, as indeed she deserved to do.

'The Little Flower of the Flock'

Though our mother was certainly vain (and had a good deal to be vain about) she was not at all conceited, and was well able to laugh at herself. Therefore she enjoyed it as much as we, her children, did when she told the story of the day when some unknown visitors came to Clairmont Gardens, when she was barely two years old. 'And who is this wee person?' said one of them, bending over the small, stout, pink-cheeked figure. 'I am the Little Flower of the Flock' she replied with every confidence.

Whence this strange nonsensical phrase emanated I have no idea, but probably from one of Nuck's stirring Baptist hymns which she would hum as she went about her work, and always accompanied the measured tread of her long, narrow, feet as she came along the corridor to the nursery. Wherever it came from, the meaning was perfectly clear to everyone, including the 'Little Flower' herself and her much less fortunate elder sister, Maynie. Maynie had had a rotten life before Nuck arrived. She had been a plain and difficult baby, and didn't alter as she grew, and had, therefore, in the six years of her life, seen off five nannies.

Her problems had been compounded by the fact that when she was three a pretty, amiable, baby sister was born who was to die two years later, and the wretched Maynie was left to deal with her considerable troubles on her own as her grief-stricken parents were too distraught to notice. It was no wonder that she was handed over to Nuck's care with trepidation. In Nuck, however, she found at last steadfast love and understanding, though also the firm hand she needed and had lacked. Even the scary topic of Little Marjorie (as the baby sister was known from the day of her death) could be broached and Nuck's brisk response 'Little Marjorie is safe and happy in God's hands now, and you and I are the ones who have to do the living, so let's get on with it' was very consoling. The nightmares and tantrums gradually ceased and Maynie blossomed and became a different child.

Though she never regressed to her former wild ways, she always had a volatile, emotional and dramatic temperament to deal with, so it was extremely bad luck for her that when she was six and a half, our mother, Mollie, was born. She was born exuding charm like laser beams. As a great surprise to her little blonde mother she arrived with lots of dark hair and soon her convivial and joyful nature was clear to everyone around her.

She grew into a pretty, talented, amusing little girl, a delight to her parents (especially her besotted father) and as for Nuck – well, Nuck's heart was permanently lost on Mollie's birthday, 28 February 1897. Not that Nuck was capable of being unfair to children. She always said, and certainly believed, that she loved all three children equally (Mollie having been followed two years later by Bob). 'I love all the children *exactly* the same and as much as any soul could' she declared.

But Maynie was no fool, and though I never saw or heard of any overt jealously on her part, she *must* have felt sore. Who had ever treasured *her* first letters and drawings, for instance? And yet every single scrap that Mollie wrote or drew was lovingly glued into albums by her parents, and we were very grateful to them because when she showed them to us in years to come she and we all laughed ourselves silly over them.

Nuck, though she treasured birthday cards and valentines which children made for her – and was extremely pleased and gratified when one of my brothers, aged three, asked if she would marry him when he grew up – would never have indulged in those albums. It was far too dangerous. Far too conducive to the besetting sin of vanity. Our mother told us that if she ever, before a party, asked Nuck if she looked nice, she would receive the reply 'Nobody will be looking at you, dearie, so it doesn't matter' or 'If you look nice in the eyes of the Lord that is all that need concern us'.

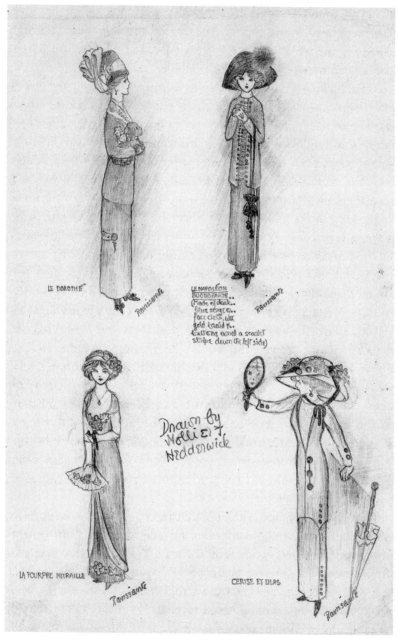

LE DOROTHÉ

Renaissance

LE NAPOLÉON
BUONAPARTE..
(Made of dark..
blue serge..
face cloth, will
gold braid th..
buttons and a scarlet
stripe down the left side)

Renaissance

LA POURPRE MITRAILLE

Renaissance

Drawn by
Mollie
Hedderwick

CERISE ET LILAS

Renaissance

Drawn by Mollie Hedderwick, aged eleven.

A generation on, she still battled on our behalf against this sin. Once we were all in the nursery while a kind aunt read us a story and I, sitting at the table with its green bobble-edged cloth, was opposite the mirror. Into which I glanced. Only a fleeting glance but Nuck saw it, and snatching up a rug from the sofa, held it over the mirror, obscuring it, until the story came to an end, looking at me the while in sad reproof. No child ever got away with a transgression and good behaviour was acknowledged but not too much. (Vanity again.)

So it was amazing, considering how just and uncompromising she was, that she managed to spoil Mollie and Bob so much. Maynie escaped her undiluted influence because she was sent off to board at St Leonards, in the footsteps of her two elder step-sisters, at an early age. And Bob went to Fettes, so only the 'Little Flower of the Flock' had her conviction that this was so on a permanent drip-feed.

I don't know if the question of boarding school ever arose for Mollie. Probably not. Probably nobody could have borne to let her go (though it may well be that her step-sisters, loving and loyal as they were, had their reservations). Instead she went, intermittently, to Laurel Bank, where she would have received an excellent education if she had had any discipline to back up her lively intelligence. But she hadn't. Her mother wrote notes with alacrity to excuse her from afternoon school. Mollie had a headache or toothache or a cold, said the notes, but in reality Mollie didn't want to play games, or do domestic science or extra maths, so she never went to school after lunch in all her life. The notes ceased after a bit. Laurel Bank, doubtless fed up, just accepted the situation, wasteful though it was.

Nuck, a great exponent of stern and formal education, *must* have disapproved, but Mollie could and did play one adult off against another and, as always, she got her way. The result was that she emerged from school with a great love of literature and poetry (which she already had from her father), a little Latin and some French, and excellent marks for anything which involved her strong artistic talent. But no maths at all – what little she had met in morning lessons had passed her by – and no science or games or sense of her own place in society. She remained and much enjoyed, being the 'Little Flower of the Flock'. Should she ever falter in this conviction, Nuck was there, in later life, to restore it, as she lived with us when my parents married, twice a year for months at a time.

She did all the mending and ironing and looked after the four of us (and I dare say installed a bit of structure into our free and easy lives), and in between her visits there was always Clairmont Gardens waiting, warm and welcoming, if the 'Little Flower' was over-tired or troubled or just home-sick. She could shed all of us into Nuck's nursery, and be cosseted, and have breakfast in bed, and generally be indulged. Indulged is what she was, rather than spoiled. She was saved from the latter in that she found it funny, and knew perfectly well that it was outrageous. As when, at sixteen, she spotted an exquisite bureau in an antique shop and couldn't wait to rush home to plead with her father. He was at first stern, saying there were plenty of bureaux and desks in the house, she could choose one out of the morning-room for a start. He asked how much it was, and on hearing the price said 'Dearie, what are you thinking of? If you need a bureau of course you shall have one, but you really don't need a *treasure*.' 'It's a *girl's* bureau,' she said, knowing exactly his Achilles heel, 'one hundred and fifty years ago it was made for a *girl*. I want to be the girl to take care of it now . . .'.

Of course she had the bureau, accompanied by many paternal congratulations on her good taste. We would never have known this story in all its detail if she hadn't told us, and she told it, laughing at her own temerity, applauding her sharp eye and *slightly* ashamed of exploiting her beloved father.

It seems wrong to apply the word 'spoiled' either to her or to Bob, though she was certainly given much too much too easily, and he, had he not been sustained by the money his father had so assiduously made, would have lived all his life on social security. But he was one of the most lovable men ever invented, and rightly continued to acquire friends – as she did – to the end of his life, so there was nothing much 'spoiled' about him and maybe it was only sour Uncle Jack who said so.

Uncle Jack was sour because, as a young man he had had a lovely, riotous, Edwardian time in London, and his name was written on the walls of a restaurant in Soho (where Aunt Nan presently took me to dinner and I saw his name there beside Lily Langtree and Beebohm Tree and lots more) and it all came to an end with huge debts he couldn't begin to pay. His elder brother, our grandfather, rescued him from his debts and disgrace, on condition he came back to Glasgow and kept away from music halls and lived with another brother. A very nice brother indeed, merry and clever and an admirable companion, but that didn't help. Uncle Jack bore a grudge against Fate, and mourned his lost golden days all his life – though he never spoke of them, but we heard of them from other people – and had only to see a child to make an adverse comment. So maybe one can discount his views.

He said to all and sundry that Nuck was spoiling Mollie and Bob and it may be so but I don't see how it was done. She never betrayed her standards or principles, or let a child get away with misbehaviour, or escape due retribution. And it was she, after all, who applied the only discipline they had, because there was none from their doting parents.

Bob was of course in danger of being spoiled, as the only son after five daughters, but his childhood sounded like that of any normal, naughty, cheerful little boy. When he grew up he married a most interesting wife and had a couple of admirable sons, while he himself tried his hand at this and that, always with enthusiasm which soon ran out for one good reason or another.

At one point he ran a restaurant. He was an excellent cook (though he employed a chef, not wishing to be tied) and was extremely neat with his fingers, always making fascinating little objects which nobody else had ever thought of. The restaurant was in an excessively old building, with low, undulating walls and tiny twisting stairs. No room, therefore, as he had hoped, for all the huge family portraits which he, as the only son, had inherited. There was no room for them in his flat either so he was at an impasse. Ever ingenious, he soon had the answer. He cut out their heads, cut down the frames very neatly, and hung them all round the restaurant walls.

Many of them had been three-quarter, some full length, and they went back as a family record for two hundred years and more. When

I first saw familiar kindly old Grandmother Hedderwick (born 1789) minus her billowing black sleeves and quiet folded hands over which the muslin streamers from her cap had fallen so gracefully, I felt as though I were at an execution. Only her large, plain face peering out of the disproportionately heavy frame . . . And her husband Robert looked as though his head was sitting in an eggcup, having been sliced off just below the chin, so that the edges of his white stock formed a rim.

Vandalism though it was, Bob was himself, his unique self, and nothing at all like his clever, industrious, cultured, father or his earnest and efficient mother. It must surely be a good thing to be able to be oneself, even at such a cost to the family portraits. I don't think he ever harmed a living person in all his life, and he was certainly unaware of harming portraits of dead ones. In his view he had kept all their faces, and remade the frames beautifully and that was all that mattered.

Our mother, beloved over a long marriage by our father and all of us, did of course miss the 'Little Flower' fix when Nuck, and then her mother, died – her father had died long since. In spite of all our father's efforts, she had an unadmitted dream that there was still someone out there who would buy her *Vogue* and chocolates and tell her she was beautiful ten times a day.

Time went on and after a long illness my father died, and the 'Little Flower' was on her own aged seventy-two, with a lot of friends, children, grandchildren and great-grandchildren all loving and admiring and all at her beck and call but, as we well knew, unable to supply the missing element. It came from a most unexpected quarter. A quiet, scholarly, reclusive man had adored her from afar for years. He had never known family life, as a child of very elderly parents and childless himself, but he took to her teeming progeny as to the manor born.

I could swear she never mentioned *Vogue* to him but he took out a subscription at once, and chocolates galore lurked about the house, and he never stopped telling her how beautiful she was, watching her across a room with sheer delight, of which she was well aware. They had ten wonderful years, and when he died, it was soon clear that, among the many things he had taught her as she blossomed as the 'Little Flower' all over again, was how to survive his death. She did this with nobility and courage, sustained by the knowledge that if he, who was so wise and learned, thought also that she was the 'Little Flower of the Flock', it must indeed be true, as she had always hoped.

'Tubbins'

My mother's family name, Hedderwick, is a good one and sufficiently unusual to be traceable back over many centuries, although it is confusing that the Hedderwicks seemed unable to think of any boys' names except Robert or James (always one or the other for the eldest son) and, if pushed, John and Alexander. Generation after generation after generation.

A Robert and a James were recorded in 1539 and most of them seemed to be around Forfar and Edinburgh until the end of the eighteenth century, when a Robert made the great trek west. This Robert, when married, had two sons (and guess what they were called . . .) and sired the Glasgow Hedderwick clan. They weren't much more original when it came to girls' names – Jean and Margaret, Jane and Mary. But in 1804 a James, then aged twenty-two, married a seventeen-year-old Joanna, thereby introducing a name which remained in the family and is at the moment borne by one of our daughters, who fortunately likes it. Her forebear, the seventeen-year-old bride, met her James when she was a child and was playing peevor, a version of hopscotch. A big boy had kicked her peevor away and run off with it just as James Hedderwick was passing by. James pursued the thief, punched him and brought the peevor safely back to its tearful owner, and so began a friendship which resulted in marriage and thirteen children. Robert, James, Alexander, John, Jean, Mary, Jane, Margaret, and then they had to add David, George, Charles, and Flora and William. 'Joanna' was reserved for a granddaughter.

'Peevor Robert's' son took his entire family to America, seeking the much-talked-of opportunities there, but it was not at all to his liking, and they all came back to Glasgow as fast as they could. He went on to found a printing and publishing works and the *Glasgow Citizen*, and in due course became printer and publisher to Queen Victoria and so carried the Royal Warrant.

On his death his brother became editor of the *Glasgow Evening Citizen* and also published several books, including one of unreadable poetry. One can't help feeling none of these would have seen the light of day without the advantage of the publisher's name and address (James Hedderwick & Son, Melville Court, Trongate).

It may be that the dearth of imaginative names encouraged the Hedderwicks to use nicknames and pet names. Certainly the habit was rife when I was born. The eldest daughter was seldom called Grace. She was 'Gaick' or 'Gaickie'. Anna, her next sister, was always Nan. Then, Grandad having married Granny thirteen years after his first wife had died, their first baby was called May, but was always Maynie. The next two, Mollie and Bob, were known as 'Mowser' and 'Bowser'. I haven't the least idea why but I have no doubt there was some cosy, amusing, reason behind it.

There was, however, nothing cosy and amusing about the nickname Maynie acquired, and which remained glued to her for life, as she (rather ruefully) records in the rose-tinted memoirs she wrote in her old age. She must often have felt that Fate had it in for her, such was her misfortune even in details as trivial as this.

Her first six years, until Nuck came and reigned over the nursery with steadfast love, had been wretched for the plain, tempestuous, unhappy little girl. It was a bad start, and though Nuck soothed her and straightened her out as well as she could, more bad luck waited in the wings. She had pneumonia twice, and pneumonia in those days was a solemn business. There was nothing to be done for the patient but allow the disease to take its course, and the course was via 'The Crisis'. If you survived this you lived and if you didn't you died, and everyone knew that, and the fear and anxiety were potent and well-founded. Maynie survived twice, but it made her mother extremely anxious about her, so she was over-fed and over-cosseted and by the time she was sixteen was not only still plain, but stout as well.

'Coming out' – when a girl put her hair up and emerged from the schoolroom into adult society – had a very different connotation in those days. That was all it meant – that on the morning after your seventeenth or eighteenth birthday you were expected to be, and behave like, a grown-up, no matter how you felt within. Maynie, at sixteen and 'half-out' (which meant you could attend informal dances and dinner parties but not formal white-tie affairs), felt miserable within.

Because her mother was so nervous of her catching a chill she had had high-necked, sleeved, evening dresses made for the poor girl, at the time when everyone wore wasp-waisted low-cut dresses with tiny sleeves or only a froth of lace where a sleeve might be. Maynie, after wrestling with her limp, mouse-coloured, hair – an extra affliction in a family where everyone else's hair was of interesting colour and texture – and clad in her long, solid cream-coloured satin dress decorated with pearls and tiny silver bugles, entered the drawing-room nervously before a dinner party one evening. She was hailed by the son of a family friend, who said loudly 'Well, sweet Tube, how are you now?'

From that time on she was 'Tube', and then 'Tubbins', but 'Tube' was much in use all her life.

She was intelligent and musical, and an excellent cook having daringly taken a course at the 'DO' School, which was an original thing to do, and almost revolutionary in the days when few of her school-fellows ever contemplated doing their own cooking or would wish to. To her, though, it was a skill she – and all those at her table later on – enjoyed to the full. She had, however, to contend with an emotional and easily inflamed temperament, and her need and desire to be loved (although she was both loved and loving) was forever getting her into all sorts of trouble. She was an ideal aunt. Enterprising, affectionate, completely non-critical, with a tremendous capacity for enjoyment, but even a young child could recognize her vulnerability, and feel protective towards her.

At a time when girls, with luck, married very young, she didn't. Mollie, her junior by nearly seven years, almost beat her to it. Then she married Gerald, a dedicated naval officer, after meeting him only four times, but in those days people married for life, no matter what, and so they did. She followed him to Malta and the China station, and shared with him his bitter disappointment when he, who had been in the Navy since he was thirteen and had had a splendid career including a DSO (he was to acquire a bar to it in the Second World

War, though already elderly and supposedly unfit for service) was axed in the decimation of the Navy in 1919. He then bought a farm, as this seemed to him the best way of being able to keep hunters, and in this he was right. They had two daughters, Anne and Ruth, who rode before they could walk and who, by the time they were ten and twelve were adept at training Dartmoor ponies to sell on as suitable mounts for young children. They certainly *were* suitable too. My brothers and sister and I used to look on with awe at the training sessions.

Anne and Ruth would rush up behind a pony and slap its hind-quarters (it must not kick) or swing down from the saddle and hang on to the girth under its belly or fall off sideways over its neck (it must not move or step on its rider) and all sorts of other hair-raising tricks. They were very good at this, and also at the actual dealing, in which Maynie took no part. She couldn't bear to look on at the training sessions either, and no wonder. They scared the daylights out of us, their cousins and contemporaries, though we were no strangers to horses. Or, perhaps, because of that.

Gerald, however, was doing much the same thing with his horses, schooling them and selling them, so there was a good deal of stern commercial conversation in the house, very unfamiliar to our unworldly ears. He was a short, square man with a large, noble, head, and a mischievous smile (which told no lies – he was a fearful tease) and a short temper. The whole mood of the house was turbulent to say the least and it was not all due to him.

Maynie had had a lot of theories from the moment her daughters were born, the salient one being that a child had equal rights with an adult. Therefore, when asked to do anything, Anne and Ruth were positively encouraged to ask 'Why must I?' or 'Why should I?' and then there would be a long discussion, Maynie starting off very quiet-voiced and calm and then becoming more and more exasperated as the children produced better and better arguments against doing whatever it was until it all turned into a full-blown furious row. And all about 'Don't come in here with your wellingtons on' or 'Do be an angel and fetch me a few apples from the larder'.

The result of this régime was that there were four people, all with equal rights, and all very different desires and demands, and only one of them – Gerald – felt that there was something wrong about this in that he, as breadwinner and *pater familias*, should have some sort of authority over somebody. But he hadn't, and was always outnumbered, so he felt at bay, and blew his top more often than he need have done. Maynie always reacted and the children came in on one side or the other and it led to a thoroughly volatile life.

Until, that is, the day when Maynie came across a doctor who could only be described as alternative. He explained to her that men, as well as women, underwent a menopause, and that Gerald was suffering all sorts of hormonal changes and couldn't be expected to keep calm. But *she* must, no matter what he said or did, and in addition must administer to him, with a glass of water, a couple of these pills whenever he was in a rage. She was exemplary in her efforts but somehow they only made matters worse. To be confronted with a sweetly smiling face instead of the usual pink furious one when he felt he had a grievance drove him beyond the bounds of reason, and to be offered a pill and a glass of water – a glass of *water* of all things, only to be tolerated when brushing his teeth – was the last straw. There were many broken tumblers. Fortunately she couldn't keep up the calm-in-the-teeth-of-the-storm régime, and attempts to do so, with the pills, were quite soon abandoned. Those few weeks had, however, done nothing for his dignity, and left her with an all too familiar sense of failure. She had tried her very best, and she had failed and life was back to its usual pattern.

I was there on one never-to-be-forgotten occasion when he and she were having one of their long, loud quarrels. Once I had said to her – boldly for a ten-year-old, but to her one could say anything – 'I do *wish* you and Gerald didn't fight so much'. '*Fight*, darling?' she said. 'We don't *fight*! We love each other much too much ever to fight! In fact, we are a byword all over the county for how much we love each other.' On this particular day the demonstration of their marital love was taking place in the usual manner, and so loudly that one felt that this, too, must be known all over the county.

I sidled from the room and took refuge in the drawing-room, which was always bleak and sunless in the morning so nobody ever thought of entering it. This time, however, I was soon followed by Gerald, who banged the door behind him, flung himself into an armchair and roared 'GOD, what a woman she is! How can *anyone* stand her!' I curled into a corner of the windowseat, trying not to be there, pretending to read *Horse & Hound*. The door was flung open again and Maynie stood there, pink-faced, out of breath, her large bosom heaving under her hyacinth-blue jumper. 'There, Gerald' she cried 'I've been to your study and I've poured water on your fire and I've drunk your whisky, so THERE!'

There was an electric pause. I couldn't even breathe. Then he let out a great shout of laughter and she, tentatively at first, laughed too and then we were all laughing till we were helpless, and he was kissing her enthusiastically between renewed spurts of laughter and I expect many of their banging, violent, rows ended thus. But not all, and any two family members could line up against any other two at any time, so the politics of the house were hard for an outsider to follow and the equal rights theory meant that there was *never* mutual agreement.

Maynie, however, had found a *modus vivendi*. Confronted with an adverse situation she simply repainted it in her mind in the colours she would have wished it to be. Not exactly denying the threatening reality, just altering its texture and colour to be more congenial, and carrying on from there as though that was how it truly was, and, for her, it was so.

Enormous problems and sorrows lay in the years ahead, and she survived them, and not because she didn't suffer. She mitigated her suffering and made it bearable, so was able not only to survive but to enjoy her life. Gerald died, and so did Anne, and Ruth lived in Australia, and Maynie lived from year to year on Ruth's promise, never to be fulfilled but steadfastly believed, of coming home for Christmas.

Not so long before she died I deserted my husband and children and went to spend the night with her in the once noisy house. She was, as ever, a loving and enthusiastic hostess, and she made our dinner á deux a party, cooking a duck to perfection, and opening a bottle from Gerald's still stocked cellar. She was full of eager interest in both my life and her own and I left next morning grateful, refreshed, and full of admiration. What did it matter if she distorted facts to fit her desires? She had become so good at it that it was as though she had a cocoon of rose-petals wrapped round her mind, and when death came to her it was swift, with a stroke, and she was by chance at that moment with an adored grandson, so that for once her heart-felt desire and the reality were at one.

The White Shoes

I have an unfair advantage. In my mother's nursery time had stood still, so that her childhood had joined ours without a break, and I knew her Edwardian childhood as well as I knew my own because, in the nursery, it was unaltered.

The nursery was on the second-to-top floor of a large hushed, grey, Glasgow house, and over it Nuck still reigned, as tall and dignified as the house itself. She distributed love and astringent discipline, clean clothes on Sundays, hot milk and Huntley and Palmer's tea biscuits as she had done all her life, and it was she who stood in the doorway and turned back Time should he ever have the temerity and stamina to climb the long stairs from the pillared marbled hall to the nursery floor.

Whatever changes took place in the rest of the house over the years, the sanctuary of the nursery remained inviolate. It was a great relief to us, arriving in the holidays, not only to find the carriage clock on the corner shelf hiding its elegance in a worn leather case, but to know it had always been so. We liked having the same tall fireguard, with the extra brass rail for airing baby clothes, and we liked the shelves full of time-honoured books, accepting the ones we liked and the ones we loathed, as we accepted people, through propinquity.

We liked knowing that the oval table, with the green bobble-edged cloth, was the same table and cloth which had sheltered our mother when, overcome with pity for the fate of a new little brown loaf, she had taken it and hidden under the table to save it from being eaten. With or without a brown loaf, we hid under the table and peered at passing feet from under the serrated canopy.

The frames of the tall, double-glazed windows were painted in a peculiar terracotta enamel of excellent quality which had withstood two generations of children without a chip. (The strange colour puzzled me for years but recently I read that there was an Etruscan vogue about the turn of the century, and I can only think our grandmother fell victim to it.) Both generations of children looked from the same tall windows over the same wet dark street, with the fascinating oblongs of light from the windows opposite, and the same sing-song sound of the trams passing at the end of the road on their way to Charing Cross. And if one group of children saw carriages and cabs pass by, and another cars, that was a mere detail, because the real world lay inside the nursery, and not outside in the rain. The double-glazing of the day and night nursery windows was a tribute to our progressive grandfather who had this added as far back as 1901, the year that Glasgow trams abandoned horses and became electric.

He also installed bathrooms on all three upper floors of the house, and had one put in the basement, too, for the maids. He took no notice at all of his friends at the club who said, 'For heaven's sake, man, what do maids want with a *bath*?'

He must also have been a pioneer with electricity, for the light switches – domes of sectioned brass like little peeled oranges – must have been among the earliest light fittings of all. This brass, which fashioned not only the light fittings but undulating three-legged bedside lamps with frilly japsilk shades, and a fascinating up-and-down pendulum above the brisk white china shade in the nursery, was an excellent shock conductor.

Several of the lamps could not be turned on without a curious furry sensation up one's arm and in the nursery pantry one could, by turning on the light with one hand and the tap with the other, experience quite a sharp electric shock. One of my brothers overdid this and wept, but Nuck did not sympathize. She simply told him it was a daft game to play and to get on and eat his tea like a Christian.

She made tea in the nursery pantry (all our other meals were carried, on vast japanned trays, up those interminable stairs from the basement kitchen by a little kitchen maid in a print dress and an engulfing cap and apron) and boiled the kettle on a gas ring, and cut banana sandwiches, and poured into a tall jug the town milk which always tasted to us slightly odd.

If people came to tea with us treats were added to the normal tea – cookies from Skinner's, glossy like newly peeled conkers, and little square cakes iced in a particular soft icing, pink or white or pale yellow. We were excited one day to be told that our admired and adulated older cousins were coming to tea and would, moreover, have tea with us in the nursery. We were fully conscious of the honour, though I now realize there must have been a strong adult lobby against allowing us to seep downstairs, since I was four at the time and my brothers younger.

To mark the splendid occasion I was to be allowed to wear my white buckskin shoes. They were exquisite shoes, like a pair of white mice, but they were seldom worn because they were party shoes and I was rapidly growing out of them. I thought about wearing my white shoes at the tea party during all my waking moments, all the following days. When the day at last dawned it didn't dawn at all. The whole world was obscured by a dense black Glasgow fog.

Glasgow fogs differed from present fogs or Los Angeles fogs or London pea-soupers of postwar fiction in that they were black, black like coal, black like the darkest night except that no light could penetrate them. They invaded the house, creeping in round closed windows, hazing the light bulbs and covering everything with a pall of grime. Unwary children, scampering across the bedroom in bare feet, were rewarded with dark grey soles, and a book left open in the morning had gritty pages by night.

However, the messenger boy from Skinner's bicycled through the blackened street with the cookies and cakes for our tea, and Nuck said, 'Well, well, all's well'.

But it was not.

My throat had begun to ache, and all too soon I couldn't swallow and could hardly speak. I tried to cry but it was too painful, so I was shut inside myself, my misery and me. Nuck said, 'Poor wee thing. You've got the fog in your throat. It's no good giving you a jujube because you wouldn't be able to swallow it. Never mind. You'll be better tomorrow.'

The afternoon was several years long, and my efforts not to cry were as agonizing as the desire to cry itself. I still could not believe that this had happened to me and was sure that by teatime, when they came and I had my white shoes on, I would be better.

When it was time for us to be washed and changed for tea, grown-up voices agreed it would be silly for me to put on my white silk party dress considering my sore throat, but I was told consolingly, 'Never mind, you can wear your white shoes'. Squeezing them over my stout fawn wool socks only matched the general distortion of the day, and I was not surprised when no healing magic from my shoes crept up my legs after all. At tea I sat between the huge cousins, and they were joking and kind. 'Are you not eating your cookie? Shall I cut it into wee bits for you?' 'Here, have a pink cake to match your hair ribbon.' I tried to say I couldn't eat, but no voice at all emerged from my swollen throat. 'She's got fog in her throat,' voices explained over my head. 'She'll be all right tomorrow.'

What good was tomorrow? Tomorrow Marjorie and Dick and John would not be here and I wouldn't be wearing my white shoes and the treat would have passed me by. Outside the window was the dense and muffling blackness of the fog, only stirred by the faint fog-horns of the ships on the distant Clyde.

Inside, in the bright cosy room, with the foggy haze around the light like the corona round the moon, everyone laughed and talked unmindful of me. I sat, my chin not far above the edge of the white tablecloth, unable to eat or speak, enveloped in sorrow and my hugely aching throat, and my white shoes were no consolation at all.

Driving

It was lucky for us that my brother and I, at two and a half and three and a half respectively, didn't live in the age of instant and intensive journalism. Otherwise how would our discreet and respectable families have coped with the inevitable headlines?

'Rector's children poisoned by arsenic!' 'Cook attempts to murder children!'

So it was, but as it was, in the early 1920s, it happened, it passed, it was over, and all my brother remembers of the dramatic event is the horrors of the white glutinous tonic, called Benger's Emulsion, on which we were fed as we recovered.

He has no memory of the confusing night, when we were snatched from our warm beds, rolled up in tartan rugs and driven in my father's draughty little car to the ever welcoming house in Glasgow where our grandparents lived. It was a second home for us, this house where we had all been born, but a strange way to arrive that night with all the grown-ups in terror or tears, and everything mysterious and frightening.

I suppose it was lucky we got there, even after escaping the arsenic poisoner, because my father's cars tended to be dodgy. This particular one had started to belch smoke one day when only my mother and I were with him. He stopped, we all got out in a great hurry, with him shouting 'Keep well back! The petrol may explode!' and, though I wasn't sure what explode meant I ran down the road holding my mother's hand, completely infected by her fear, while she called over her shoulder 'Keep away *yourself*, you silly thing!' as, fearless and heedless as ever, he hovered to see if he could deal with the fire himself, presumably with his bare hands as he had of course no extinguisher.

The fire died away, however, without igniting the petrol and if we didn't proceed with that journey we certainly did with many more before we reached the heights of a sure and steady bull-nosed Morris Oxford which never went on fire and whose doors, once shut, stayed shut. (On this car my father had a little rail fixed to the running board to make it safe for his dog Kim, who preferred to ride shotgun rather than inside.) This time, fortunately, we reached Clairmont Gardens without further misadventures. It was just as well. Everyone had had enough for one night.

David and I had, for weeks, been ill at intervals, and we were strong healthy children and nobody could understand why we were ill so often, so thoroughly and together. In those days small children were not offered grown-up food – there was no question of our learning to like shellfish or curry or game or zabaglione – and our baby brother was not yet on the boring food we ate, so the doctor deduced that something in the nursery food was upsetting us. As indeed there was.

He came thundering at the door at half past ten at night and charged into the house saying 'Get these children away! Get them out of here now, tonight! I've just had the results from the analyst and it is arsenic.'

David and Rosemary, aged two and three.

44

It transpired presently, when my parents and the police had been able to piece it all together, that the recently acquired cook, who had come with excellent (albeit false) references, had a long history of mental disturbance. Outwardly normal and calm, she had conceived a passion for my mother, and felt she would have more of my mother's attention if David and I were out of the way, and she very nearly succeeded in the latter objective. It was really no wonder that my mother took a scunner at that house, as this was not the first drama which had occurred in the few years we lived there.

Eighteen months before this the plump and cheerful table maid (in those far-off days even families who considered themselves permanently strapped for money as ours did, could have, without surprise to anybody, two resident maids) had not felt well at midday and gone to lie down. The cook – not the poisoner, but a former, normal cook who left to get married in a very proper way – told my mother that she had sent her to bed, and my mother said 'Quite right. And do tell Jessie just to stay there till she feels better.'

But Jessie reappeared at teatime cheerful as ever, and brought in the tea tray with the silver teapot and the Italian Spode china and all the scones and cakes and cookies – how *did* people eat so often in those days? The kind cook, meanwhile, went upstairs to make Jessie's bed, and let out a piercing shriek. In the bed there was a dead baby.

I don't know the fate of poor Jessie, or what she had intended to do next, but I seem to remember muttered adult conversations about Jessie being all right now, home with her mother and brothers and sisters, so I take it no dreadful retribution fell on her via the law. But for my mother, who was only twenty-five and had three children (and another one to come very soon) it was dreadfully upsetting, although could not compare with the arsenic episode.

Safe in Clairmont Gardens we both eventually recovered and we were promised that when we were well we could go to Lyon's toy shop in Sauchiehall Street and choose anything we wanted. Absolutely *anything*. We were sustained by this thought as we swallowed our Benger's Emulsion. I don't know what David wanted but I knew what I wanted more than anything. A pedal-car. Simple and puerile by today's standards – just a little car you could sit in and propel by pedals under the dashboard, and drive about the garden or landing. The best ones were very realistic with tiny doors (though one could easily climb in from the top), and the few simple dials which dashboards had then were faithfully reproduced.

One fine and exciting day it was decided we were well enough to go and choose. Lyon's was a treat in itself. On the ground floor there were small toys, pocket-money toys, lead farm animals (we were ardent collectors and would save up for a calf for a favourite cow, or a little black piglet) and jumping beans and, at Easter-time, delicious ducklings from China. They were real ducklings, crudely stuffed, fragile and ephemeral, but while they lasted we loved them ardently and at 6d each, could afford them with a fortnight's saving.

It never occurred to me, and nor did it appear to occur to the grown-ups – not even our fiercely animal-loving Aunt Nan – that this was a cruel trade, breeding ducklings to kill and export as cheap, short-lived toys. We simply loved them for their feel and their wonderful colours, shading subtly from cream to dark amber, and their endearing, individual faces. Each Easter we took ages selecting the one we thought the best.

Young children have all their senses at the ready, not yet blunted by time and tide, and the tactile sense is an important one. The ducklings whose frail bodies came into our family did not endure their brief lives entirely in vain, so vividly do I remember the delight of stroking the satiny head and soft, downy breast. We made careful nests for them, and gave them crumbs to eat and water to drink (the lids of Milk of Magnesia bottles made admirable drinking bowls) and loved them till they fell to bits. And then, resolutely, we tried to concentrate on *next* Easter.

On the ground floor there was also a cage of mechanical song-birds, which sang for a penny. This was a very great temptation when one had saved up 4d for a good drawing pencil – red Royal Sovereign or green Venus – or just enough for a farmhorse but never, of course, a penny extra. This time, however, we passed dazedly through the glories and temptations of the ground floor, where the tiny overhead railway bearing cash from the counter to the cashier was a diversion in itself, to the first floor where the big toys were. We had seldom seen it. It was well beyond our ken. Dolls houses and amazing elaborate forts and bicycles and cars and pony-and-traps on wheels and wheelbarrows and scooters and small-sized garden tools and wigwams.

The last was familiar to us. Our beloved Aunt Nan had sent one for our previous birthdays (David and I, a year apart, have birthdays on successive days) and it had arrived in a most exciting package. Long and thin – about 5 feet long in fact – the wigwam was wrapped round a plank of wood, and there was also a Red Indian suit for each of us. David as a (small-sized) Big Chief, had a magnificent headdress of coloured feathers a foot long all round his head and down his back, to go with his braided and beaded brown cotton suit. I, as his much larger squaw had a brown cotton top and skirt with no beads, and a band of braid to tie round my head with one black feather sticking up. All very authentic, no doubt.

Aunt Nan came down from Glasgow for our birthdays and we greeted her with reminders about thanking her for the lovely present ringing in our ears. David rushed eagerly forward, saying 'Thank you *so* much, Aunt Nan, for the lovely plank of wood'. It was a portent. Though he was quite happy to play Red Indians in our beautiful wigwam, a good piece of wood was, and has re-mained for him, much more valuable.

It didn't take me long to locate the cars on the first floor. Over them hung a sign saying 'for 3 to 6 years old' so I should have had a good choice. Not that I havered – I saw the right car at once. Brown, with black lines outlining the body and doors, all very restrained and realistic which the cars painted in primary colours were not.

There were not, in those days, any brightly coloured cars on the road. Cars were black or brown or grey, though when the King ordered a maroon Daimler everyone said 'What kind of a colour is that?' but soon found out and copied him. There were also a few, very few, dark green cars and I was told that, before I was born, Uncle Bertie had had a very smart car striped in dark green and black but I never saw such a thing.

My moment of joy was short-lived. I couldn't fit my legs into the car at all, no matter how I tried, so I couldn't pedal it. Sadly I tried the crude red and blue and yellow cars, all in vain. Not one allowed for too long legs, even the ones which were really long and lavish and had little low, slanting dashboards. I felt it scarred my life, though I dare say it was character building as most disagreeable things are. David got the little brown car which he drove about the garden with panache, and I had a bike with little tiny wheels, called a 'Fairy Bike'. It must have been designed by some clever parent to use up as much juvenile energy as possible, because the wheels were so small that one had to pedal like a maniac to get up any speed at all.

My father was forbearing, however, and took me with him one day when he bicycled along the road to the bank. Emerging from there we saw a small boy briskly running away with my 'Fairy Bike'. My father said 'After him, Kim' to our gallant and ever-ready dog, an order which Kim carried out with great effect, sending the little boy yelling, bikeless, over the horizon and returning with a piece of the boy's shorts in his mouth.

Perhaps it was the disappointment over the little brown car which led to my passing my driving test on the morning of my seventeenth birthday, driving around Hillhead and doing three-point turns somewhere near the 'DO' School, with a dour examiner who never questioned how I had learned to drive in a few hours.

The fact was that I longed to drive, and had a father who was honourable and law-abiding to a degree, except that he felt there were a few areas of the law which didn't apply to *him*. As I had grown to my full height at fourteen and could pass for the extra three years, I had been driving him around since then in our big, old family Rover, with double-declutching and all that caper taken for granted. Traffic was, of course, lighter, but roads much worse, narrower, with no helpful things like Cat's-eyes to aid the headlights which were mere candle-power compared to today's blinding beam. However, I enjoyed it. My father liked company and I liked driving. We didn't mention the fact that it was subversive but we both knew it was.

Once, when I was fifteen, I drove him to Cornwall to play golf. I drove him each day to the club house, drove away, walked the dog, swam, read, painted and generally enjoyed my solitary day, and at the end of it went back to fetch him after he had had time to play two rounds.

Perhaps, if I had fulfilled my desire to drive at three and a half, my enthusiasm would have become dimmed and I would have missed all these pleasures, so maybe there is something in the exasperating old saw that 'Nothing is for nothing'. Even arsenic poisoning.

Germ Warfare

Professor Lister, when he defined for the public the existence of germs, never had a more ardent disciple than my Glasgow grandmother. I suppose the knowledge was a new theory in her youth, but it was clearly right up her street, and germs were, for her, a lifelong menace and challenge. She never let them be out of her mind, never let herself be deflected from the battle, and could never see the shining, rosy skin of an apple without seeing the invisible germs swarming all over the surface. She could hardly wait for you to give the dog a pat on the head before saying anxiously 'Off you go and wash your hands, dearie, he's full of germs!'

Other lucky children could crowd round the Italian ice-cream vendor at the gates of the Kelvingrove Park, and buy sliders, but never us. 'Think of the germs!' Exquisite homemade ice-creams on their special little glass plates were, of course, a treat, but perversely we knew that a dripping yellow slider at the park gates would be a better one, despite the germs.

So the germs became our enemies as well, if for different reasons, and the battle against them really only surfaced when we were staying with our grandparents in Clairmont Gardens. (In our much more casual life at home germs were never mentioned, and doubtless rife, but we were four very healthy children so no doubt we and the germs had learned to live together.)

One summer when I was six and my two brothers and sister all younger – indeed, Joan was a baby – our parents announced that we were going to have a summer holiday not in Glasgow. This was strange indeed. We always, and without fail, went to Glasgow for all holidays, weekends, birthdays – ours and theirs – and any other excuse that could be found, and we loved it and could think of nothing better.

I can't imagine what took my parents, but we were at least to have a few days at Clairmont Gardens *en route* for a mysterious Criccieth, where we were to stay in a boarding house and the landlady would do the cooking when my mother had bought the supplies. When we reached Glasgow and these plans were recounted to my grandmother, her inevitable reaction was 'I do *hope* the landlady has a clean kitchen. Kitchens are such a harbour for germs if they are not kept scrupulously clean.'

Her own kitchen was kept so clean that it was more like an operating theatre. It seemed to me to contain little except the huge range, and an enormous table scrubbed to a bone-white, and a bleak, unsmiling cook with colourless face and hair who was never in the least pleased to see us when our grandmother took us down to the kitchen while she ordered the menu, for a 'treat'. No germs could have emanated from there, but my grandmother's fears of the invisible enemy were justified. I don't know which of us started to cough first that summer, but in the end, we all did, and it takes a very, very long time for four children to incubate and get through whooping cough. The result was that we never got to Criccieth – we never got further than Glasgow.

All that long summer, until the hard-working doctor at last convinced our grandmother that we were germ-free, we were confined to the nursery floor of the tall house, and not even allowed to go out to play in the Square Gardens (to which all the residents around it had a key) in case we cast a germ, in passing, through the closed bedroom door of our frail old grandfather on the floor below. If it was hard for us, it must have been insufferable for the grown-ups. Used to a quiet house they had to endure thundering feet overhead since whooping cough doesn't make one feel ill for a large part of the time, and we had a lot of energy to expend.

Nuck was the one grown-up who certainly didn't mind it at all, as she delighted in having her nurseries full of children, whooping or not, and in any case she was deeply in love with my younger brother. He was three, and had asked her to marry him when he grew up, and she had accepted with pleasure. He loved the John Gilpin poem, and so she read it to him patiently and endlessly, day in and day out, and he never tired of it, and my next brother and I couldn't escape it. (We have both since decided that our characters were warped by being unable, ever since, to hear the words 'John Gilpin was a citizen of credit and renown' without being overcome by feelings of fury and exasperation.)

There is not, thank God, much whooping cough about now, but there was a child whooping away in the waiting-room when I went a few years ago to the surgery. When I went in to the doctor's room I told him he had a splendid case of whooping cough coming in next and he said 'Oh, have I? Wonderful! I've never heard what it sounds like.' It sounds bad enough, and feels a lot worse, as the coughing fits seize you and go on and on and on, far beyond your endurance and often culminating in being sick. I remember our younger brother, Nuck's fiancé, sitting up in bed, looking very small in the large bed, and at the end of a coughing session gasping 'Am I going to die?'

For physical activity all we could do was play tag or hide-and-seek, but of course we soon knew every single possible hiding place. We raced along the green-carpeted landing, into the bedroom at the end of it, then through the big stately bedroom where we had all been born, its dressing-room and bathroom, and then the nursery bathroom, before we returned to the nursery pantry, the night nursery and the day nursery – where, of course, Nuck would be nursing the baby and reading 'John Gilpin'.

The nursery bathroom, whose fittings had been closely overseen by our imaginative and practical grandfather many, many years back, was brilliant. I have never to this day seen such a well-thought-out bathroom. The basin was wide and shallow and set into a big marble table, and had its own mini shower on an elegant brass stalk. This was perfect for washing hair and washing baby clothes, and – since it was set low – for small children to wash themselves. (The last must have been a trial to tall Nuck, but she was never one to complain.) The bath, encased in panelled mahogany, had a tall hood to enclose the shower, and a set of about ten brass taps shaped like daisy heads, along the back edge of the bath. These were to provide fine, sharp, Jacuzzi jets of water from all parts of the bath and shower, and allied to the soft, silky Glasgow water, baths there were a luxury whose equal I have never met since.

Otherwise we would be in the nursery, playing ludo or snakes and ladders, or drawing and painting and trying to persuade Nuck to read something other than 'John Gilpin'. Fortunately, we could draw happily for ages. Our mother had brilliantly discovered how to take four children anywhere and everywhere – to the dentist, the hairdresser, out to tea with friends, on train journeys. Just give them each a drawing book and expect them to get on with it. We used hard-covered exercise books with unlined pages. They had green covers and red spines (on which we wrote our names to avoid confusion), and we drew steadily through them, one page after another, in our very different styles. Mine were tedious, looking back on it. I only ever drew people. The boys were much more varied, and our little sister, when old enough to have a drawing book, never could draw, but did so imperviously and very happily just the same. Our drawing books were very important to us and like an extra limb – we must have filled several each during that summer.

We had no visitors as everyone, encouraged by our grandmother, was afraid of the plague. Even the cheerful little kitchen maid, who normally brought the nursery meals upstairs, had to leave them on the floor below for Nuck to collect. In vain she protested that she had had whooping cough. Our grandmother was taking no chances. Our mother had to go home at last to look after our long-suffering father. (It must have been a trial for him, fond as he was of his parents-in-law, to have his wife and children flee to Glasgow at every spare moment.) And it is to Nuck's eternal credit that I don't remember her ever losing her patience with us throughout all those long, long weeks. We certainly did chafe against our imprisonment, and once my brother David bravely crept halfway down the stairs to the floor below, just to see the world from another angle, and our grandmother came out of her room and saw him. 'Oh, go back! Go back, dearie!' she cried piercingly. 'Think of the germs!'

Only two brave aunts came to cheer us on. Aunt Nan played cards and dominoes with us, and Aunt Grace, known as 'Gaickie', brought a most wonderful present, two huge volumes of out-of-date Army and Navy catalogues. Within their red covers one could find every object under the sun, carefully illustrated with accurate pen drawings, and we pored over them endlessly, completely fascinated. Toys and tents, guns and billiard tables, linen, china, pots and pans and kitchen stoves, meat safes and plate covers (Britannia metal 5s 6d. Tin 1s 6d). Toothpaste and fly-whisks, silver tea sets and jewellery (carved jade earrings set in 9-carat gold £2 10s). Clothes and shoes and books and Bibles. We made long bizarre lists and then looked them up and they were all there. We coloured in some of the pictures, very carefully so that they looked quite real, but only David and I could do this as Nuck's fiancé was not old enough to do it properly.

So it was with the greatest possible sorrow, when at long last we were well, and any idea of Criccieth had long since gone as had the whole of the summer, that we were told we couldn't take the Army and Navy catalogues home because they were going to be burned – because of the germs . . . So were all the books we had read and touched and, of course, our drawing books. We were outraged at this, immediately considering certain pages to be of the utmost value, but the law was the law and they all went, including my mother's copy of 'John Gilpin' with the original Caldecott illustrations. As Nuck packed them into a big cardboard box her Aberdonian common sense for once overcame her discretion.

'What a silly caper,' she said. 'What a daft waste.'

Lister and his germs had a lot to answer for.

Losing Mademoiselle

My mother married at twenty and then had four children within six years, a situation which my well-ordered Glasgow relations felt to be unbridled. Nobody ever said anything, of course. Family love and loyalty prevailed above all, but a normally generous and fair-minded aunt, who had given each of the first three babies a silver mug as a christening present, could only bring herself to give the fourth a horn spoon. My grandparents gave all possible help and support (consistent with the preservation of everyone's dignity) and when my father was given a parish in Gloucestershire and we moved down there and out of reach, the help took the form of a warm welcome in Clairmont Gardens for every moment of every holiday.

My mother, of course, turned back eagerly, several times a year, from being a hands-on mother to being the beloved and indulged daughter at home, parking us in her unchanged childhood nursery in the care of her equally unchanged nurse, and we loved it as much as she did. We loved the decorum and predictability of life in their hushed house, which was such a contrast to our normal free and casual life.

We loved the cosy, loving tribe of Glasgow relations – the warm welcoming aunts and uncles, and admired older cousins, and even the alarming old uncles, living together in bachelor content in Oakfield Avenue, surrounded by fascinating paintings and objects, and talking above our head in deep growly voices.

The house waited for us, tall and warm and quiet, everything exactly as we had left it, from the rubber outside doormat with my grandfather's initials on it (little recognizable fragments of it survive today) to the calm refuge of the nursery, with Nuck in control of her domain and of us. When we arrived there would be chicken soup and sandwiches waiting in the dining-room. If my father was with us there would be a decanter of whisky as well, casting a tawny glow on the shining surface of the table. My grandmother clucked around us, saw that we were fed, and sent us up the long green-carpeted stairs to Nuck, and bath and bed.

The first Glasgow night was always exciting and it was delicious to lie listening to the rain, and the singing sound of the trams at the bottom of Elderslie Street, and distant ships hooting on the river. Also to think about the next day because our first treat, and one we could hardly endure waiting for, was to go to the Art Gallery. We knew it well from our earliest years, and had been brought up on stories of the days when it was new, in our mother's childhood, and I think we thought, as many Glasgow children must have done, that it was *our* gallery, because it was as familiar as home. As the years went on, however, our ever-considerate grandparents felt our mother needed a rest from us, so they engaged someone to take us out into the park to play. It was in the late twenties, when I was about eight and the

others all younger, and the unfortunate lady hired to take us out was French. The idea was that we would learn some French by osmosis (a forlorn hope if ever I heard one). But I don't suppose we listened to a word she said. Walking along beside her in stout Harris tweed coats, topped with berets for the girls and matching caps for the boys, our objective was set from the moment the front door had closed behind us and we let it be known we were going to the Art Gallery. 'Ze art what?' she cried. 'No, no! Zis is not exercise!' 'Oh, it is,' we assured her. 'It is a huge place,' and we swept her along by the most direct route.

The park was all very well, and we knew it intimately, every path and pond and fence and shrub and statue and waterfowl. We were very fond of it, but the real point of the park was that it led to the Art Gallery. Mademoiselle hadn't a chance as we raced her along the paths and over the bridge where the wooden planks were wide enough apart to see the opaque, scum-surfaced waters of the Kelvin speeding below us. (Very alarming, this. No matter how often one told oneself that no child could ever be thin enough to slip through, it made the bridge seem fragile and we always felt triumphant to be safely over it.)

Over the road, and soon we were there, at the wonderful great red building. Up the wide steps through the heavy doors, and into the enormous hall, then crowded with sculptures. All our familiar friends. Rodin's Thinker, ever wrestling with his insoluble problem. Laocoön and his sons desperately tangled with serpents. Adam and Eve, and one we called 'The Charioteer' but I don't remember a chariot, just a bronze man straining back against his plunging horses. Nymphs in ghostly marble. Venus de Milo with her neat little breasts and massive hips. Gods and goddesses by the score and noble-headed marble men with curly-edged leaves unaccountably attached. We each had our favourites and were delighted to see them again.

We knew exactly how to lose Mademoiselle. We knew every corner of the Art Gallery and we just melted away in different directions. One to model ships; some beautiful yachts, some liners sliced in half so that one could examine the exquisite tiny detail of cabins and boiler rooms and lifeboats. One to see the wildlife cases, where rather moth-eaten exotic birds clung to their dusty branches, or animals in dramatic poses thrust balding legs through the jungle. I always went to the far end of the hall and crept up the stairs to the painting galleries (hiding behind the marble balustrade until I was out of Mademoiselle's sight), and our small sister would tag along with any of us and enjoy it, a capacity she never lost in later life, being extremely adaptable.

I don't think there was much rehanging in those days. I always knew where to find the pictures I wanted first to see. Whistler's 'Carlyle' looking (so I learned much later) far more congenial than he ever did in life. The 'Marriage de Convenance' with the drooping young wife, bored out of her mind, at one end of the long formal dining table, and at the other her elderly husband absorbed in his dinner. And the 'Knight in Armour' looking so thoughtful and romantic. There were the exciting paintings by Hornel and George Leslie Hunter, and among the daring new acquisitions Peploe and Cadell and Fergusson. I remember standing entranced in front of Cadell's 'A Lady in Black' when it was a new and exciting arrival. Either 'The Orange Blind' had not arrived then or I hadn't found it; it was an unforgettable moment when I did. I would stand in front of these paintings for ages, examining them minutely. I didn't know what I was looking for, but the colours in the white tablecloth in 'Le Marriage' fascinated me, and the shine on the helmet of the 'Knight in Armour', and this colour beside that in Cadell and Peploe. I pattered from one to the other, peering to see how the colours were disposed.

In retrospect, I am overcome with remorse when I recall the glimpses of the distraught little lady, hurrying through the corridors and galleries, and in and out among the glass cases and suits of armour, desperately seeking even one of us. Her little tight plump coat, her jaunty hat and shabby defiant high heels all now make me anguished, in retrospect, as I visualize her impoverished and gallant figure. She had no means of knowing we would foregather in the hall when it was time to go home. Children didn't have watches in those days, but there was a clock, and I knew it was my job to round everyone up in good time, which I did. We had been heedless of her, simply vanishing into thin air, avid to renew acquaintance again with our favourite treasures and never for a moment considering her anxiety and responsibility, and I am, belatedly, much ashamed.

We were all there in the hall among the sculpture, innocent as the dawn, when she, distressed and red in the face, came click-clacking across the marble hall. We waited for retribution but none came. She was a little less jolly on the way home but that was all right by us. Soothed and satisfied by our fix of pleasures in the Art Gallery we were content to think about all we had seen – and presently to begin looking forward to tomorrow's visit. For we all realized now that play in the park, and exercise, and fresh air would last each day only as long as the walk to the Art Gallery took, and by tacit agreement none of us said a word to the grown-ups about our nefarious activities, not even our very small sister.

Mademoiselle continued to be nice to us, to labour with a few French words, and to be relentlessly jolly. At the end of the holidays she invited us to tea in her tiny bedsitting-room, somewhere off Woodlands Road. She and our sister sat at a little table on the only two chairs, and the rest of us sat in a row on the bed, and she gave us lemonade in waxed paper tumblers and delicious, cloud-soft sponge cake from Skinner's, while she made a pot of tea on the gas ring in the corner. She laughed and talked in her rich fluting voice, joking about the contrivances and compromises of cramming all her life into such a small space, and I do hope we managed to convey to her something of our appreciation. It was a shame about the French – there really wasn't time to absorb much in the brisk walks to and from the Art Gallery – but what lasting joy she bestowed on us, morning after morning, as she sat reading her novel on the bench in the marble hall, and let us free among the pleasures and treasures which have enriched our lives ever since.

Lessons from a
Glasgow Girl

It makes me feel like a brontosaurus to admit it, but I have had painting lessons from one of the Glasgow Girls.

It is true that I was six years old at the time, but Miss Agnes Raeburn didn't seem to be so very old, being one of the flat-fronted elderly ladies of the time who, in the twenties, wore long flat cardigans over silk blouses, and long flat tweed skirts. Her cardigans and skirts were often of an indeterminate grey-brown, to match her hair, but the quiet discreet ladies of her ilk all seemed to dress in what one would now think of as Armani colours. Off-centre colours. Blue-grey, grey-green, greenish fawn, and so on, all understated, and all worn with absolutely *no* make-up, or hairdresser hair.

Of course, at six, I had never heard of the Glasgow Girls, and I imagine this group of talented artists and craftswomen were not then so defined. Nor, for that matter, had I ever heard tell of the Glasgow Boys, though their enjoyable paintings were familiar to me in family houses and on the walls of the Art Gallery, and I knew who they were. I had certainly never heard of Miss Raeburn as an artist and wouldn't have been particularly impressed if I had. Our mother had been a student at the Glasgow School of Art, and we four children were all expected to draw and paint until the cows came home, and we did and we loved it. (We thought everyone went on like that, and it was a great surprise to us, as we grew older and emerged into a wider world, to find this was not so.)

Miss Raeburn's name, however, was a familiar one in the rôle of long-standing family friend, and I cannot bring myself to refer to her except by the formal title by which I knew her. I only knew her first name by default, as it were, and it would be unthinkable to call her 'Raeburn' in the crude, coarse fashion of present journalism. (Even writing this sentence makes me feel embarrassed.) It was to her that my grandparents had turned for advice when my wayward and talented mother, Mollie, had wanted to leave Laurel Bank – to which excellent establishment she had only paid half-hearted attention – and go to the School of Art at an early age. And I was used to hearing grown-ups say 'Oh, we'll ask Agnes' and 'Agnes Raeburn will have that address – I'll telephone her this evening', and so on. I can see my Aunt Nan, my mother's much older half-sister, returning from lunch at the Lady Artists' Club and hanging her Burberry in the huge press at the back of the hall and saying over her shoulder 'Oh and I had a nice chat with Agnes Raeburn, mother. She sent you her love and asked so kindly after Mollie.'

So, spending yet another holiday in our grandparents' house near the Kelvingrove Park, I didn't take much notice when my mother proposed asking Agnes Raeburn to give me painting lessons. I was in the room when she telephoned, lying on the morning-room floor painting sunsets. My mother had just shown me how. You wet the paper all over, and then put on successive washes of colour, fading down towards the horizon, and then you had to wait, with considerable impatience, until the paper was dry enough to add a rich orange sun sinking behind a range of purple mountains.

Completed sunsets were scattered all around me and I was enjoying myself, listening with half an ear to my mother's conversation. Miss Raeburn's gentle voice over the telephone was perfectly clear and she was

not at all enthusiastic about the idea. 'Oh *no*, Mollie dear. I really don't think I could. I don't teach, and I know nothing about children. I really *couldn't* teach a wee girl.' My mother's protests that I was not a wee girl were echoed by my indignant mutterings from the floor. Nobody thought of me as a wee girl. I was tall and stalwart and already the eldest of four, a fact of burdensome responsibility which grown-ups emphasized at every point.

So I was in no sense a wee girl, and kind Miss Raeburn, badgered and beguiled, agreed to give me some lessons. She lived on the other side of the Park, and as my mother and I walked along the familiar paths – past the elaborate circular fountain hung with iron cups on chains for thirsty children and from which we yearned to drink and were not even allowed to touch, and over the bridge with its frighteningly wide-spaced planks under our feet – I felt considerable trepidation on that first morning. I knew I was an imposition, and was nervous about such unknown territory as a painting lesson.

Imposition though I was, Miss Raeburn was extremely kind to me. She was right when she said she knew nothing at all about children, so she didn't treat me as a child and I found it very peaceful. The only concession to the many years between us was that, when we had a mid-lesson break, she had tea and I had milk (Glasgow milk was fairly horrid compared to the country milk we had at home but we never said so, to each other or anyone else because Glasgow had its own glamour and this encompassed everything, even the milk.)

During the break the biscuits and conversation were shared equally between us, though we didn't linger long as we had work to do. We didn't work in her studio, but in a sitting-room, with a view from the window of a bridge, with traffic going over it and trees whose fragile spring green was hard to capture.

I sat at a table covered with a brown bobble-edged cloth, and Miss Raeburn sat beside me, drawing. She had long pale hands which could draw a line with an assured mastery that even I could recognize. First I had to paint a bowl of polyanthus. Miss Raeburn gave me a sheet of thick, superb paper, rough as a pebble beach, and a large brush with an exquisitely fine point – the sort of brush, I now know, which is made of the very best sable and which would, today, need a second mortgage to subsidize its purchase . . .

She pointed out to me the shape of the arrangement, and how the light fell, and showed me how to mix three different shades of purple, but when I shifted over, expecting her to demonstrate as well as explain the painting of a leaf, she said, 'No, dear. You and I paint in our own ways. This is your painting and you do it and I will not touch it.' (Many years later, when the paintings I had done under her eye surfaced, I was thankful to remember her saying this, otherwise I would have thought them not all my own work. I was *amazed* at how good they were, if depressed that I seem to have made little progress since.) She taught me to look or, as she put it, 'to look *properly*', which is the first essential for any aspiring painter.

From her I learned to look and evaluate and compare and take nothing for granted, so that perspective and tonal values and composition were never a worry – or at least not a worry in themselves, and worrying is far too small a word for the struggles and agonies involved in painting a picture. I don't know how many lessons I had, but I do remember very well my eager anticipation on our subsequent journeys across the Park. I can feel now the surge of pure pleasure when she showed me how to hold a horizontal pencil, and so discover the exact angle of the picture-rail running into the corner of the room. I had been wrestling with it in vain, unable to reproduce on paper what I saw, and when she showed me how to find out – how to look *properly* – I felt as though I'd been given a present.

And, of course, I had. Miss Raeburn's life had been devoted and dedicated to art so that her knowledge was distilled and pure and she taught me more than she knew. It goes without saying that I did not and could not know her character and personality, having only had a child's-eye view of one aspect of her, but in that aspect must have been something of her essence, since her impression on me remains so clear.

I have since wondered how she would have fared in today's climate. From today's viewpoint her life was limited and narrowed in spite of her talents and achievements, and even these were qualified by being a member of a group who were to prove themselves influential, but of which she was only a modest part. There were, of course, feminist stirrings in the background. The suffragettes had already made their political point, but there was still a very long way to go before women were clamorous in their demands for personal fulfilment in every direction and all at once. Try as I will I cannot fit her into this scenario. She must have had many frustrations and disappointments on the way along, but however she managed her life and her art, she preserved her certainties in the latter, and I was lucky enough to catch a glimpse of them, strongly recognizable even to a six-year-old.

A few years ago I came upon an exhibition in the Art Gallery in celebration of the Glasgow Girls, and there I found Miss Raeburn again, in the huge-sleeved blouses and flowing, nip-waisted skirts of her youth, and I gazed at her kind and gentle face with considerable gratitude and affection. She taught me so much and so enriched my life, because the delights of painting outweigh the tortures, and that's for sure. In due course I followed in the footsteps of Miss Raeburn and my mother, and went to the Glasgow School of Art (the best then as it still is), so I was very fortunate as a student. And a student I remain, and will do so until my last breath, albeit always in debt to those who set my feet on this exasperating, exhilarating, desperate and fulfilling path.

Thank you, thank you, dear Miss Raeburn. I was very privileged and I never forget it.

On Strike

My father loved his Glaswegian parents-in-law, and they loved him, in spite of his obvious drawbacks. He was, after all, not only English and Episcopalian but, even worse, an Episcopalian minister.

His first parish, however, when he came out of the Navy at the end of the First World War, was Ardrossan in Ayrshire, which was excellent news for everybody. It was near Glasgow, so that coming and going was easy and constant, and a parental eye could be kept on my mother, who kept on having babies. She went home to Clairmont Gardens, and her own bedroom and her own old nanny in her own nursery, for each birth until she had delivered four of us within six years, a deplorable fact since a rector's stipend fell far short of what was needed to keep such a household afloat. Also, in time, the house at Ardrossan became too small, and it was time to move on.

Finding the right living for a priest is not easy now, and it was not easy then, but in due course my father was offered a couple of small parishes in deepest and most rural Herefordshire. The Rectory was a huge, beautiful, Queen Anne house with which my mother immediately fell in love. Practicality was never her strong point. All she could see was this marvellous house, and acres and acres of garden for all her children to play in, while my father's enchanted eye took in the excellent and extensive stables and the several fields which went with the Rectory. He was a wonderful horseman, and keeping horses in those days, in the country, cost very little. (Not that he ever thought of whether he could afford something or not – that wasn't how either of my parents operated, so their financial affairs were always fragile in the extreme.) So they accepted this living, and arranged for the removal at the exact time that the General Strike of 1926 was due.

After many months of unrest in the mines and elsewhere the Trades Union Congress had organized a nationwide general strike to bring the country to a standstill, which in the end only petered out because a number of people, who had other priorities, volunteered to drive buses and trains and shift supplies about the country. But that took time. Initially the Great Strike, as the TUC called it, worked. It was well organized and doubtless the exact time of the start was kept secret, but even if it had been public I doubt if my parents would have taken any notice. They were both optimists in quite different but equally zany ways, and their eyes were fastened on the great adventure of moving, not only far away to England, but to what was, for my mother, a completely different way of life.

Though she had holidayed in the country, my Glasgow-born-and-bred mother had never lived there, and wherever she was, had all her life been surrounded by every creature comfort. Even when her father had, as was his habit, rented a huge country house for the summer and filled it with all their relations, her mother had been able to order all she needed each day from her usual shops in Glasgow, which was sent down to the country by train.

My mother was aware that she would have to make many adjustments. For a start, the big beautiful Queen Anne house had no telephone. Nor was there any telephone in either of the parishes – which each consisted of a little church and a few hundred people scattered over many fields and woods, with neither shop nor pub – except in the squire's house, the Court. The squire was the patron of the living, and he was as strange to this office as he was to the status of squire, being in reality a retired factory owner from Birmingham, with little knowledge of, or sympathy for, country ways. As my father set about accepting the living and assessing the pros and cons, he asked the squire if he would install a telephone in the Rectory. The squire said no. He said that in an emergency we could use his telephone 'as the two houses were pretty well next door'. In that there were no houses in between, only the church, this was true. And the two drive gates were less than half a mile apart. But the Court drive was more than half a mile long, and ours was also a long one, so it was as well that in the event nobody had to run this course, especially as the Court drive was uphill all the way.

Lack of a telephone, therefore, had to be accepted, as my father certainly couldn't afford the cost of having one installed and, after all, his parents had always done without. My maternal grandparents, however, had not. Not only did my progressive Glasgow grandfather have one of the first-ever telephones put into his house but, practical and imaginative as ever, he had several, to save people having to run up and down stairs whenever it rang. He also had an internal telephone system put in so that the nursery floor could communicate with the kitchen, the drawing-room with the top floor, and so on. (Children were not allowed to use this, so it constituted, for us, one of the few attractions of being adult.)

Thus, in moving from sophisticated Glasgow to backward Herefordshire, my mother faced a shop-less, telephone-less life with understandable trepidation, but, to her credit, nevertheless found great joy in country life, and all might have been well had it not been for the water supply. The Rectory depended for water on an exceedingly erratic well. This problem was a pleasure to the squire, whose factory made components for such things, and he was happily back on familiar ground when he promised to install the very latest Artesian well. 'I know what it's like with kiddies and you've got four of 'em. You' got to have water. Course you have. Trust me.'

It was all too easy for my father to trust people. This wasn't the only time his trust was misplaced. Not only did the new Artesian well fail to produce water exactly as the old basic well had done (often the only water we could get had to be carried from a farm many fields away in little zinc tanks either side of a pony's broad back), but it was of a very dubious quality when we could get it. The drinking-water, left standing for an hour, developed little orange sponges in the bottom of the jug, and all the family except me got boils which took years to be cured. When my mother sent a sample off for analysis she was told the water was perfectly healthy, so we were then left to drink the little orange sponges and be thankful when we had any water at all. One of my brothers was so well trained in water-conservation that, showing a visitor to the bathroom, he said, 'When you've washed, leave the water in the basin for the next person and don't pull the plug unless you absolutely *have* to.'

At the time of the move, however, the unforeseen water problems lay ahead, my parents were young and adventurous and eager for that new life. Our Glasgow grandmother did not share their confidence. It sounded to her the wildest and most dangerous place in the world. Hearing that the Rectory drive gate opened on to the road – as drive gates tend to do – she had a large notice painted 'Caution! Children!' and made my father promise to nail it up. Obligingly, he did, but he had lived in the country most of his life, and knew that there were roads, like this one, along which cars very seldom came in the 1920s. As for us children, if a car was heard in the distance, we would pelt down the drive to catch an excited glimpse of it if we were quick enough. In addition to the notice by the gate (which we children found humiliating, 'as if we were *tigers*' said my brother scornfully), a huge hamper also came from Glasgow with supplies from Cooper's for the day of the move. Our considerate grandmother found it hard to visualize being 7 miles from shops, unable to telephone, and dependent on only intermittent calls from a baker and a butcher, and a nearby farm from which we could get milk and butter and eggs. (Once or twice, when a cow had just calved, the milk was pink which we found rather fascinating, though it drove my mother to distraction.)

When the three large removal vans at last rolled up the rutted drive, the brisk and efficient men soon had the first one unloaded. Fortunately, it contained kitchen things and the Cooper's hamper. 'Aye, we get things the right way round,' said the genial foreman. When they began on the second van, my mother hovered anxiously. Since antique furniture was the cheapest on the market at the end of the First World War, when my parents had married, all their furniture was old, much of it beautiful, but almost everything missing a hinge or handle or beading or a piece of inlay, and in a fragile condition. The removal men, however, were experienced and skilled, so eventually she left them to it and went to sort out the kitchen.

The second van was half unloaded, with two or three arm-chairs sitting about in the drive, and an elegant (and hideously uncomfortable) Regency sofa poised by the front door steps, when it happened. As if at some magic signal, all activity ceased. The men left everything where it was without a word, and retired into the van. Silence fell. My parents looked at each other and wondered. Tea break? Lunch break? When the silence from the van had continued beyond any reasonable rest period, my father went to investigate. After what seemed an interminable time, he returned to my mother and said, 'Poor chaps. The strike has now begun and they can't do any more work.' 'What do you mean, *can't*?' said my mother menacingly. 'Well, you see', said my father reasonably, '*they* have jobs and *their* firm is a decent one, but that is not so for many of their fellow-workers, and our chaps have to support them. Of course they do. I feel really sorry for them. Stuck out here. So far from home. What a predicament. Poor chaps.'

After some hours the foreman came to the back door. One look at my mother's expression killed any idea of asking for a cup of tea, and instead he asked where the nearest pub was. 'As far as I know', said my father, concentrating on trying to light his pipe, 'Leominster.' 'And that is how far?' asked the foreman. 'Ah, got it . . . About 7 miles, I think' came from behind the cloud of smoke. There was a long pause. My mother continued to unpack china and stow it in cupboards, and at last the foreman said with a gallant attempt at confidence, 'Well, right then. We'll just take the van then.' 'NOT with my furniture in it,' said my mother, whose voice matched her furious eyes. 'Yes, well, the empty van,' said the poor man, retreating a step. 'It is blocked by the half-empty one,' pointed out my mother, 'and so it must remain if you cannot move any more furniture.'

The foreman melted away. By now the sky was threatening and rain would soon be falling on the armchairs, and the Regency sofa in the drive, but for some reason my mother's brow had cleared, and she stopped unpacking china and turned her attention to the Cooper's hamper. From its thoughtfully assembled depths she brought out ham and pressed beef and cheese and butter and oatcakes and fruit cake and shortbread and Sally Lunns and raspberry jam and everything else my grandmother had thought that they might like and the removal men might need, and she set them all out on the table, with the teapot all ready, and the jug of milk from the farm, and she waited for the next move. It was a while in coming, but towards evening an understandably nervous foreman came again to ask if they might have a cup of tea? By now all sweet reasonableness, she said, 'I *wish* I could give you one. You must all be so thirsty, and hungry too, and I am so sorry, but my husband has been explaining to me about the principles behind the strike, and I absolutely see the point. Unless everyone is solid it will fail, so I won't let you down. I am solid too and I am as much on strike as you are.'

His eyes upon the laden table behind her, the foreman shifted uneasily and then muttering that he must talk to the lads, he vanished again. Silence returned, faintly broken by the sound of rain beginning to fall. Dark rainspots scattered on the Regency sofa's shabby blue brocade cover, and the men stayed in the dark van and my mother waited in the kitchen.

Presently the silence receded before steady and determined footsteps through the house, and welcome sounds of 'Back your way a bit, Dougal', and 'Whaur's this yin for

then?', and my mother made the tea and went to tell the men it was ready. As they all sat round the kitchen table and the bread and cheese and ham and pickles vanished like snow in the sun, accompanied by pot after pot of tea, the men said they'd have the van emptied that night, and the last one by tomorrow forenoon. My mother said earnestly, 'No one need ever know that we all started the strike twenty-four hours late. Need they? There is nobody else here after all, and no neighbours to watch us, and I won't tell a soul about you, and I am sure you won't tell a soul about me.' She smiled at them. 'Will you?' Gazing at her, their mouths full, they nodded in admiration and agreement, every one of them.

The Ride

When Mrs Preston came to call on my mother, she came spanking up the long, weedy, rutted drive to the Rectory in a troika, drawn by three exactly matching strawberry-roan ponies.

It was an impressive ensemble. She was a tall, heavy woman with smouldering dark eyes, a fur hat, and a set, unsmiling mouth. Presumably she hadn't much to smile about, being a white Russian who had fled before the Bolsheviks in the classic manner, with her baby son in her arms and jewels sewn into the hem of her coat. She now lived in a village about 4 miles from ours, breeding and selling roan ponies as a meagre means of livelihood for herself and two sons. It can't have been a very profitable venture, albeit in horse-mad Herefordshire, which might have explained Mrs Preston's cheerless air, but this was not of immediate concern to me and my younger brothers and sister. It was our reluctant mother who had to take her into the drawing-room and spend an uncomfortable half-hour with her.

There was never any mention of Mr Preston, but her sons had come with her – Frederick, impressively wearing long white flannel trousers, as he was old enough to be at his public school, and Boris, at nine a year older than I was. We were pleased to see other children as we so seldom did. We were very happy in our remote, not to say isolated, surroundings, and played most interesting games, but there was no doubt that visitors were a highlight, never mind the matching ponies and the extraordinary vehicle.

Frederick was tall and good-looking with a tanned skin and dark eyes, and he looked us over with what appeared to be amusement – rather superior amusement. This, fortunately, soon abated. My brother suggested a tour of our unbelievable grounds. The disadvantages of our beautiful Queen Anne house – the fact that we had no means of warming even one room properly, or of extracting water from the recalcitrant well – didn't show from the outside, and though the grounds were neglected and overgrown, they were extensive. It took a long time to walk from the house to the walled garden or the shaggy tennis court beyond it, and there were the remains of long laurel walks, laid out by a Victorian rector. These still provided an excellent basic road system for games of cowboys and indians or 'Don John of Austria riding to the war' and so on. The Preston boys at once saw the potential. 'We could play it on horseback!' they said. We said, well no, not really as we had one old, obdurate pony to share between us. 'That's all right', they said, 'we've got lots. We'll bring over an extra couple and then we can have a great time.'

Snowball, our pony, was old and knew every trick a child could play on her and was always one trick ahead. She made it very clear that games involving cantering up and down the laurel walks and round the back of the kitchen gardens through a jungle of brambles

Frederick show jumping.

for no purpose were not for her and perfectly ridiculous. She took action. One learned to hold on very tight when near the entrance to her field as she would suddenly swerve in, throwing her rider, with any luck, into the hedge. So mostly the Prestons brought enough ponies for us all, and Snowball regarded us as we rode past her gate, with a sardonic and triumphant eye.

In the games, Frederick, at fourteen, was naturally the leader, and I usually found myself at his side. He had very grand manners, and when we at last arrived back at the house and my mother gave us all lemon squash and biscuits, he was very polite to her, and always considerate to me. All the same, she frequently became fed up with the Preston boys and all the roan ponies, and would speed the boys out of the front door, telling them it was high time they went home. While Boris pottered off down the drive on his pony, leading one or two more, Frederick would nip round to the back door to pull off my wellingtons for me. Not my brother's or sister's wellingtons, just mine. Then he would mount his pony and trot off after his brother. Presently he took to lingering a bit, sitting on the step beside me, talking, mostly about all the wonderful estates in Russia which were his by right, and one day he was going to reclaim them. Sometimes my mother found him there ten minutes after she had ejected him, and was suitably exasperated.

I suppose this continued all one long summer. Certainly the nettles were at their formidable height because now and then our games suddenly took a turn which was, for me, mortifying. The boys would all gang up against me and canter up and down the paths, slashing at the nettles with canes shouting 'Slaughter of the Rosemary-ites! Slaughter of the Rosemary-ites!'

My feelings were deeply hurt because I didn't know what I had done wrong. I now know that what I had done wrong was to be born female, though I had never been at all conscious of this disadvantage, and our parents treated us all alike at that stage. But time passed, and presently it was only the younger boys playing 'Slaughter of the Rosemary-ites', Frederick riding peaceably beside me talking about his land and forests and rivers in Russia, and how wonderful it would be when he regained his inheritance. I knew very little about Russia, but what I had heard – snow and starvation and Bolsheviks – didn't sound attractive, and I asked him if he was sure he would enjoy the life there. He said, 'Of course. So will you. I am going to take you with me.' I said I hoped he would change his mind before he grew up, and he said earnestly, 'I'm not waiting till I grow up. I mean now, soon. I have it all planned.'

I have never in my life felt as adult, and so in control as I did then. How did he truly suppose he could get from Herefordshire to Russia himself, never mind with a reluctant eight-year-old in tow? What would he do for money? He never had any pocket money, and the meagre discomforts of the Preston house didn't augur well for stealing from the housekeeping purse. Careful of his frail male ego, I said wouldn't it be better to wait until he was old enough to earn a bit of money for the journey? 'Don't I earn it?' he flashed. 'Don't I work every spare minute of every holidays with these damned ponies? Grooming them, mucking out, feeding them, showing them, shoeing them, taking them all over the place for shows and trials? The only time I ever get off is when I come over here and have fun. I earn it all right. I just don't get paid. So I shall sell a pony and give my mother a wrong figure and keep a small profit. I've been tempted before but now I have a good case, to have you in Russia beside me when I take my rightful place.'

'Good gracious me,' I thought, 'how his brain does spin.' But aloud I said I was sure it was time they went home. So he went, calling over his shoulder, 'I'll tell you my *detailed* plans tomorrow.' 'What plans?' asked Boris. 'Nothing to do with you,' said Frederick, trotting on ahead.

Next day, however, there was a change of plan. The Prestons' man brought a note from his employer, saying that the boys were too busy to play that day, and so would they be tomorrow, as there was a most important show on Saturday to which six of their ponies were going. Frederick had to take three ponies to be shod, and Boris had to school a pony for the show. Since Boris couldn't do it, could Rosemary go with Frederick to the blacksmith, riding the third pony, as she felt he shouldn't lead two on the main road. He would pick me up at eleven when he had done his stable work, and we would be back mid-afternoon. The man waited for a reply as neither the Prestons' house nor the Rectory had a telephone. I thought it would be fun, and so did my parents, so we set off according to plan, sandwiches in our pockets, for the blacksmith 6 miles away.

It was a pleasant September day, glittering cobwebs hanging in the hedges as we rode by, and Frederick unfolded his plans for the journey to Russia. He would come for me about midnight, leaving the ponies halfway down the drive on the grass, and we could get to Cardiff before anyone discovered we were missing. Any boat would do as long as it got us to Ostend or somewhere like that, and he could work our passage. Help in the galley was always wanted, and he could cook very well as his mother had never learned how.

He could, in fact, work his way across Europe, he said – cooking, cleaning, riding and caring for horses, teaching English, and once in Russia there would be such a welcome from Katya, his mother's old nurse, and so on, and so on, and so on. I just let him talk and he was very happy to do it. I hadn't mentioned it to my mother, partly because I thought it too silly to repeat, and also because I recognized that, however lunatic his dreams sounded to me, to him they were a lifeline and therefore had to be protected. In the event, it was just as well I had held my tongue.

When we reached the blacksmith we found the forge closed. His wife came out of her cottage and said her husband was ill and hadn't been able to work for the past ten days. Any thoughts I might have had about turning home were swept away when I saw Frederick's despairing face. 'I *must* get them shod. She'll be so furious if I don't. I have no choice!' The woman said the nearest forge was about 10 miles further on, so there was nothing for it but to ride on. Frederick kept saying, 'They just have to be shod. I can't face her if I fail to do it.'

We were both tired by the time we reached the next blacksmith and he was just about to close down for the day. Seeing our faces, however, and hearing how far we had come, he not only relented but gave us mugs of tea which were most welcome, our sandwiches by then being a distant memory. It was long past the time we were supposed to be home, and it seemed to take ages to make and fit all the little shoes. We sat on a bench in the red glow from the furnace for a long long time, with the odd smell of hot hooves and the sound of iron ringing under the hammer blows and the fidgeting of the restless and resentful ponies. It was dark when we led them out and remounted and set off for home.

I rode behind Frederick, following the little sparks the new shoes struck from the hard surface of the road, and fortunately few cars came by, for the pony he was leading was not used to traffic, and shied at every car. In those pre-tungsten days car lights were not good and we must have been fairly invisible. Trotting is hard when you are tired, as we all were. The ponies stumbled as they trotted gallantly on, along the interminable, invisible black road. I wondered at one point if I would simply fall off with exhaustion, but decided against that idea on such a surface.

We came to the Preston house first on our homeward journey – ours was another 4 miles on – and when at long last we turned in at the gate, Frederick's mother stood in the doorway, looking enormous against the light, shouting, 'Where *have* you been? Don't you know you were supposed to be back at four to get the tack ready for tomorrow and bed down all the ponies in good time? Boris has had to do it all!' 'I didn't mind,' said Boris, but she brushed that aside. 'I can't trust you, Frederick. You let me down again and again. You *know* how important tomorrow is and we have to leave at 8.30 sharp.' Frederick had slid from his pony and helped me down. We

both felt stiff as well as cold and tired. He said in a remote, flat voice, 'I've had the ponies shod, mother, as you asked. I'm now going to Joe's cottage to get him to bike over to the Rectory and tell them where Rosemary is so that her father can fetch her in the car.' 'Indeed you will *not!*' cried his mother, 'or at least not until these ponies are fed and watered and bedded down as they should have been hours ago. Anyway, Joe will be in *bed.*' Frederick remounted his pony with a set face and handed the reins of the other two to his brother, saying, 'Do it, will you, Boris', and rode off into the night.

I was then taken into the house by the dreadful and enraged Mrs Preston, the situation now, in some mysterious way, having become all my fault. At first she just banged about exclaiming, and probably swearing, in Russian. I sat on the stairs because I was too tired to stand any longer. Then she passed through the hall and said angrily 'Don't sit there, child. Go into the dining-room. What a time of night to expect food.'

I wasn't expecting anything except my father, and could hardly believe he would soon be on his way, but I sat, as I had been told, at the dining-room table, and was surprised to notice that the objects in the room seemed to be gently swimming about. On the wall opposite was a large painting of a younger, but still substantial, Mrs Preston, dressed in a filmy white dress, lying on a chaise longue with a large diamond star in her hair. As I watched it floating about on the wall I thought how difficult it must have been to escape the Bolsheviks carrying both the picture *and* the baby Frederick while wearing a coat with such an unnaturally weighted hem.

When Frederick at last came back he sat down below the painting, and he shimmered too, like everything else in the room. He said Joe hadn't minded being got out of bed and was on his way, and my father should be with us in about half an hour. He added 'I am afraid you will be in trouble too.' I shook my head. I knew all the trouble would be over, once I was home. He said, 'I am so sorry, *so* sorry. I would give anything – all my estates and forests and rivers and horses, I really would give them all, not to harm you . . .' and at that moment his mother came in and banged food and a pot of tea on the table, and hurled herself out again, still muttering.

When my father came my relief was so great I almost lost my grip on the tears which had threatened for so long, even though it was bliss to sit beside him in the rattling old Morris Oxford, listening to him saying, 'Just to know you're all right. God, what a relief. What a relief. We were just so worried. Didn't know where to look. Drove all about the countryside. Kept going to that awful woman but she knew nothing. Didn't care about you two anyway, just the blasted ponies. It seemed like years.'

Safe home in my mother's arms, the long, long, black ride and horrible Mrs Preston receded, and it was only in the morning that I saw the full effect of my parents' suffering. My mother had to blame someone, and she blamed Frederick, and was so furious with him that she was beyond all reason. In vain my father said, 'What could he have done?' and '*How* could he have let us know?' – that only put fuel on the fire. We were forbidden ever to speak to Frederick again or mention his name. Fortunately for us, there wasn't much question of seeing him and Boris as term began and they went back to school.

But in the next holidays there was a hunt event, where the neighbourhood gathered, and there, only yards away, was Frederick. He approached, his eyes on my mother, with an anxious face, but she swept round, shooing us all before her, saying loudly, 'You are not to speak to that boy *ever again*, or have *anything* to do with him!' I glanced back and met his eyes. He looked desolate, made a poor attempt at a smile, shrugged his shoulders, and turned away. All the way home in the car my mother went on. 'How *dare* he try to speak to me! And he never even apologized!'

'Oh, come on,' said my father, 'that was what he was trying to do and you wouldn't let him.'

All I could think of was poor Frederick going back to that cold, harsh life and bullying mother, without even his dreams to sustain him as they lay in fragments round his feet. He had good cause to be frightened of mothers, and now was as frightened of mine as he was of his own. I felt so sorry for him that had he put 'phase one' of his plan into action that night, and brought the ponies halfway up the drive *en route* for Cardiff, I might – almost – have gone with him.

Iona

It was either 1929 or 1930 when we went on our first seaside holiday. Whichever it was it was the year in which Princess Margaret Rose was born, and it was a holiday well worth waiting for because we went to Iona for the whole of August.

The Bishop of Argyll and the Isles (a title which has always seemed to me unmatched in its splendour) used to let the Bishop's House, a retreat house built either side of St Columba's Chapel, Iona's Episcopal church, to a chaplain who would take summer duty there. This meant, in my father's case, a daily 8 a.m. communion service, two services on Sunday, and usually evensong throughout the week, and anything else that was required of him. Bishop Chinnery-Haldane had founded the house in 1894, seeing Iona as the home of prayer and intending the house to be a centre for prayer, study, contemplation and quiet. Which it has remained, but I don't suppose we were the only visitors, over the years, who failed in the last aim. As an excuse, we were six children under twelve, our cousin Anne being the eldest and our four-year-old sister Joan the youngest. Anne and Ruth were our double cousins (a fact of which we were all proud) a pair of Hodson brothers having married a pair of Hedderwick sisters.

Two sets of parents and our black spaniel, Barney, completed the party, and we arrived by sea from Oban with 'big box, little box, band-box and bundle', bringing all the supplies the household would need for a month so far as my competent grandmother could visualize it. It must have taken considerable planning, considering there were no fridges then (though plenty of brisk, cold, air and wind around) and island supplies, dependent on the sea, were limited and erratic.

Granny, however, was expert at this sort of thing and she had thought of everything and even tried to allow for personal tastes. Our cousins Anne and Ruth had a lot of these but it is easier to indulge personal tastes if there are only two of you. We were four so there wasn't so much room for likes and dislikes. One of Anne's intense dislikes was for any kind of scented soap, or indeed any soap at all except Wright's Coal Tar. She not only couldn't tolerate any other soap herself but she couldn't bear it on anyone else, or anywhere near her. This taught me sharply that I could acquire an aversion quite as strong as hers, and constantly, during that otherwise blissful holiday, I would be swept by the bleak, chill, knowledge of the prospect of washing my hands before lunch, or, worse, having a bath before bed so that all of me, all over, would exude that repellent Coal Tar smell. A whiff of it now, and I am at once back in the Bishop's House bathroom, filled with repugnance at myself, clean but at what a cost.

The house consisted of two wings, either side of the chapel, each with a row of little wooden-walled cells, and the only way from one wing to another, upstairs, was via the chapel gallery. We tried to be very quiet between 8 and 8.30 every morning, but inevitably someone forgot, or didn't know the time, and scampering pyjama-ed figures flitted back and forth over the service going on below. Now and then there would be a chase, often involving Barney, when excitement overcame caution, and once, when this had got out of hand, my father decided we must clean all the tarnished church brass in retribution.

There is even a photograph of that occasion. All six children kneeling in the long grass polishing away at the candlesticks and crosses and those bulbous, narrow-necked vases so beloved of Victorians. As I learned in later life, meeting them while on the flower rota in many churches, it is quite impossible to arrange flowers in their ludicrous and contradictory shape, but at that point flower arranging was not our task. Only polishing. Dad, as foreman and head polisher, demanded a high standard, even from Joan, and as the brass was all extremely tarnished, it took us all morning. Satisfying work, however, when we had restored all the dingy objects to gleaming gold, and only shadowed, for me, by the knowledge that the only way to get Brasso off my hands was via Coal Tar soap.

Cleaning the brass. Barney, David, Dad, Ruth, Anne, Joan, Rosemary and Haro in front.

Apart from this well-deserved punishment we led a very carefree life. We climbed Dun I, and explored all the different bays, and took picnics across the island and swam in the icy, beautiful sea, sometimes with seals for company. I couldn't believe the colours of the sea, peacock blue, turquoise, ultramarine and green. I have since seen its equal around Greek islands and off the south coast of Turkey, but never anything to surpass the colours of the sea and various sands around Iona.

Mull, across the sound, seemed always to be a long, undulating, dun-coloured land in rain, whereas we were in sunshine, drenched in colour. We, of course, had rain as well, but even wet days had their advantage. It was easier in the rain to seek out little gleaming translucent bits of Iona-stone in Sandeels Bay or elsewhere, to keep always in our pockets and ensure against drowning. When we emerged shivering from the sea into a brisk wind, and had dried and climbed back into our Fair Isle sweaters, and each been given a 'chittering bite' – a biscuit or a square of chocolate – we ran races to warm us. If our mother was organizing the race she applied maternal handicapping, and Joan started far ahead of the rest of us. If our father was in charge, it was a very different scenario, and he, as a running Blue, applied professional rules and handicapping was minimal or invisible. It didn't make any difference. David always won and Ruth was hard on his heels.

If we had had any idea that elsewhere in the world one could swim in a warm sea and dry off in a hot sun, that wouldn't have made any difference either. This was our adventure and we loved it, and none of us had been brought up to much physical comfort, though we were fed and clothed and loved beyond many children's reach.

We were joined on many of these expeditions by a tall and charming young monk from Mirfield, who was an expert on birds and flowers and plants and shells, and wrote and illustrated for us many wonderful stories, in which we all played a part, including the dog, who was 'Brother Barnabas'. He enhanced our expeditions considerably, loping along with us in his brown habit, a thick rope around his waist, and carrying half our kit. We all had haversacks so we all took a share, but even so the grown-ups had quite a lot to carry even without the problem of Anne and Ruth's bottles of water. They had both been brought up in a thicket of theories assembled by Maynie, their mother, who was always determined to get it right, whatever it was. One of these involved drinking lots and lots of water, which is an excellent idea but difficult to sustain always and in all circumstances. Apparently at home in Devon, large bottles of their own delicious well water were always put first into the car, even if they were only going to visit a house a mile away.

So Anne and Ruth, complaining bitterly about how inferior the Iona water was, never moved as far as the Bay of King's without each demanding a bottle of water to take with them. There was no plastic in those days, so it was a question of two large Kia-Ora bottles full of the despised tap water, and every time we set forth, after the first few days, Maynie would say 'Will you *promise* to carry them yourselves then?' because even she was getting fed up with it. 'Yes, yes' they said, clutching their bottles eagerly. Some hope. Within ten minutes, poor Maynie, pink in the face with heat, and not as fast a walker as her sister in any case, added the two large heavy bottles to the full picnic basket, bags full of extra sweaters and Thermos flasks, and all the rest she was carrying. She usually ended up looking like the umpire at an old-fashioned county cricket match. 'Ditch the bottles' my father said to her one day in a firm voice. 'We can leave them here and pick them up on the way back.' 'I can't,' she said, 'they might need them.' 'They can drink lemon squash like the others' he suggested. 'No, no,' she said doggedly, 'they must have their water. They are used to it.'

I know it was the year of the Princess's birth because it was a shining day, and the sand wet with recent rain, and it felt entrancing to my bare feet as I wandered in the wake of the others, thinking what a silly pair of names Margaret Rose was, as though the descriptive and romantic Rose could mitigate against the boring, hard-edged Margaret. I amused myself by making up equally useless pairs of names – Hilda Hyacinth, Madge Lavender and so on – until I suddenly noticed the others were all out of sight. We were going home across the Machair and I did hope I could find my way. I couldn't even hear any voices. I began to wonder what it would be like when darkness fell, and when anybody would notice one of us was missing, and I peered earnestly at every rock or semblance of a path, wondering if it was familiar. Had we come that way? It was getting misty and I had heard about people walking round and round in unwitting circles when lost. Every little hump and hill, as I looked around, looked exactly the same. Not a burn to guide me, not a fence or gate and now the sun was hidden in mist I didn't even know if I was pointing in the right direction or had already begun circling. And all my own fault for trailing along in that abstracted, silly way . . . I was feeling extremely miserable when I rounded a big rock and there, on the other side, sat Brother Michael in his shabby brown habit. 'I waited for you' he said 'I saw you dawdling along the sand and not noticing. What were you thinking about so deeply?' I couldn't possibly tell him I had been absorbed in deriding the Royal choice of names, but I was extremely grateful to him and all the way home listened happily to his description of various mosses and ferns, with examples always to hand wherever they were wanted.

'Oh well done' said my father absently when we reached the Bishop's House, and everyone had started tea. 'Thought we'd shed her somewhere. Thanks so much.'

Considering there were none of today's rain-and-wind-proof jackets, or plastic, or hair-driers, it was surprising how well we managed with school macks and wellingtons and sou'westers. The house had its plumbing problems which, amazingly, were sorted out by our father, who was the least practical man in the world. We were all deeply impressed, and my mother said in an awestricken voice 'It's a miracle' and he said 'You are not joking. It is.' There always seemed to be enough hot water to bath us all and warm us up if we were cold and wet, and none of the others minded the soap as much as I did. In the evenings we played games, or drew and painted, or were read to, or played charades, but the last not often as our tastes diverged over charades – we loved it and Anne and Ruth hated it, which was a pity because Anne, dressed as an Egyptian queen one day, looked perfect. Though she took after Gerald, her father, in build and was short and stocky, and had also inherited his slow, sweet smile, there was something exotic about her face and her silky black hair, and she would have been the most convincing Nefertiti if she had taken it seriously. That, however, was too much to ask. Ruth didn't look at all like her sister, but more like our sister Joan. Both were pink cheeked, blue-eyed, blondes, and both, even at Joan's young age, had rich, deep voices. This meant Ruth could often be a man in charades, which greatly pleased her.

One of the best indoor treats for me, however, was early mornings with Uncle Gerald. He was one of the rare adults who welcomed junior visitors, and he had an endless fund of noble and inspiring poems in his head which he would reel off in his deep rumbling voice, setting a standard for me of how poetry should be read. No drama, no histrionics, no intrusion of the reciter across the poet's intention, just a straightforward, unpretentious production. 'The Red Thread of Honour' and 'An Arab's Farewell to his Steed' and 'The Fighting Temeraine' all purred and rumbled into my willing ears, and though it was hard to get him to talk about his adventures as a mid-shipman in the China seas, or his DSO, he would explain, in simple terms (because for him they were simple concepts) honour and loyalty and integrity, as well as what Freemasons were about and such like. He was a physical man, and had had a hard and physical education, entering Dartmouth at thirteen, and pursuing his naval career in the harsh methods of his adolescent days, with distinction. But somewhere along the line he had furnished his mind with all this uplifting rhetorical verse, much of which is therefore now stored in my internal computer.

In the Second World War, already elderly and with a damaged heart, he badgered the Navy until they let him return to service, where, from a 'safe' office shore job, he carried out an act of such amazing courage, saving an untold number of lives, that he received a well-deserved bar to the DSO he had won long since. He was a much loved uncle, and it is good that both David and I remember the four grown-ups having fun and enjoying themselves and fooling about, because they must all have worked quite hard. Our father had his parochial duties (not that he ever wanted a holiday from those) and Maynie was doing all the cooking because 'Mowser' (my mother, Mollie) couldn't cook. She could make sandwiches, however, with supervision. 'Right to the edges, "Mowser" darling. Right to the edges. It is *horrible* just to have a little bit of egg in the middle' Maynie's voice would be heard and 'Oh *darling*. *Not* sardine sandwiches in Ruth's packet. She can't bear sardine. I did tell you.'

'Mowser' must have been more bother than she was worth in many respects.

I suppose the two men must have washed up; certainly we seldom did, although it was our job, in pairs, to lay the table. Whoever was paired with Haro was in trouble, because he found it a dull job and livened it up by putting all the implements backwards or all spoons at one place and all forks at the next and so on or just snaking the whole lot about the table in a pattern. As he said reasonably, it was quite easy then to find a spoon and two forks and a knife if you wanted to. Quite often Joan bypassed the altercations this sort of lark engendered and just got on and laid the table, by herself while everyone else was talking about it.

Years later, I came back to Iona with Aunt Nan. As my mother's much older step-sister, she went back a long way in her love for Iona, having first disembarked there from her father's yacht on one of his regular cruises round the Highlands. She had been a constant visitor ever since, latterly always staying with Mrs McArthur at Clachanach, and that was our destination when she invited me to go with her, one wartime spring. We had to obtain permits from the War Office in order to cross Mull, and the journey from Craignure to Fionnphort took a long time in an old rattle-bang bus. There were few fellow travellers with us, but one of them was a young soldier, who sat near the door, clutching his kitbag, tense. He was clearly a country boy, fresh-faced and looking younger than eighteen, and I wondered if he were being posted somewhere he dreaded because all the way he looked as if he were ready to spring.

So he was, but I had surmised the wrong cause. The bus was chugging along the side of a hill, and far below in the valley was a single, tiny cottage with a thread of smoke curling from its miniature chimney and it looked infinitely distant at the foot of the perpendicular hillside along which our road was cut. The boy suddenly shouted 'Here!' and the bus stopped, and out of the cottage door ran a small, small, white-aproned figure, arms outstretched. He leapt from the bus with a roar, and flinging his kit to the ground, where it tumbled and rolled and bounced in his wake, he hurled himself down the slope, arms wide, shouting and laughing, and the sound of it was flung back at us in the wind, in rags, as the bus jolted to a start and went on its way. I do hope he came back finally. I have often thought of him and that demonstration of pure joy.

I hadn't expected Iona to be different from our previous visit and it wasn't. The abbey was not yet restored, there was no motor vehicle on the island, and owing to the travel restrictions and the war in general, there were hardly any visitors. There was a new fishing boat to be named and they were waiting for Miss Hedderwick to perform the ceremony. This she was honoured to do, though there was a slight delay since nobody had anything suitable to dash across the bows. Someone eventually and nobly offered an inch of brandy, kept for medicinal purposes, and so the boat was duly and properly named.

Aunt Nan was the best of companions anywhere, with her capacity for enjoyment, her delight in odd details, visual or verbal, and here, of course, her intimate knowledge of the island, and friends among the inhabitants. We walked and talked and read, and I climbed Dun I to look down on the little, beautiful world around me and I swam – though I can hardly believe it now – in the ice-cold sea.

One evening, as the sun was going down, we were talking after supper in the sitting-room at Clachanach and Aunt Nan, having finished one of her rare cigarettes, threw the stub out of the open window on to the wet grass outside. Something impelled her to get up and see where it had fallen and it was just as well. She gave a squeak and rushed from the house – I hot on her heels – because it had landed on the broad back of a grazing sheep. Of course all the sheep took off as we suddenly ejected from the quiet house, and I can clearly remember the difficulty of running over hill and dale and bog and burn, torn between laughter and alarm, and every now and then glimpsing the little spark of the cigarette end lying on the grey cantering wool. Every time I nearly caught the sheep her sisters all bundled round her and prevented me, but at last I was able to fling my arms round her indignant and resentful neck and hold her, among an ear-splitting chorus of ba-a-a-s, until Aunt Nan caught up and retrieved the cigarette end and made sure no harm had been done. There was a little singe on the surface of the fleece, but it was so thick that that was all. The cigarette would probably have extinguished itself, of course, but we couldn't risk it, having inadvertently used the sheep as an ashtray. As we retreated, out of breath and giggling, all the sheep turned and watched us go in menacing silence, just to make sure we were not going to do any such daft thing again, and before we were out of sight they had returned peacefully to their grazing.

Bishop's House now comes under the aegis of Argyll Diocesan Conference Centres. It now has capacity for twenty-two visitors and is much in demand as a centre for parish groups, families and casual visitors to Iona.

It has kept up with the times, and has central heating and washbasins in the bedrooms, and is a good base from which to experience the mystical beauty of Iona, which has been such a potent part of the Christian message ever since St Columba founded the monastery in AD 563. Though I am a Friend of Bishop's House (which struggles for funding as all these excellent ideas do) I haven't been back to Iona for so long. Writing about it, visualizing it, remembering what it feels like, I can't think how I have kept away.

Perhaps next year . . .

Trustworthy

In a rapidly changing world, where many of us are out of breath trying to catch up with this or that revolution as it flies past, it is soothing to consider what remains constant. Oddly enough, one of the most reliable constants is student behaviour, unchanged, so far as one can tell, from the first records.

Post-school and pre-real-life, people are at a vulnerable and volatile stage, discovering their own identity, full of passion and despair, and convinced they could put the rotten world right if only that dreary old lot in charge would move over. Though individually they may be wild and unpredictable, as a group they can be relied upon to behave exactly as they always have done, even in these terms.

It is no surprise that the grave and mystical John Donne was, in his time, elected Lord of Misrule by his fellow students at the Inns of Court, or that a sober and hard-working doctor was once a simply outrageous medical student. I don't imagine that the young men and girls now studying at the Glasgow School of Art differ much from those of my far-off student days, or indeed, those of my mother's.

I went to the GSA in 1935. My mother had been one of the first batch of students in the glorious new Charles Rennie Mackintosh building, but even before that the school had a stunning reputation, and so I had been brought up with this dream ahead of me that, one day, I too would get there. My parents were not conventional in matters of education. I had attended the local art school on Saturdays for several years, and found it hard to wait to enrol at the GSA, so they indulged me, and I was not yet sixteen when I presented myself, thrilled to be inside the building I had always known so well from the outside. The bursar, Mr Allison, took me up in a rickety lift to show my meagre portfolio to the principal. Both were kind to me, but I was aware that they found me rather entertaining in my conviction that I could do three years' work in two. I think they took the view 'well let the misguided creature try. It won't do much harm' or some such. It can't have been that my portfolio was impressive because it certainly was not.

I was, therefore, very relieved indeed to find that I seemed to be in, in spite of, or because of, the amused glances I had caught between the bursar and the principal, and I next found myself being shown around the school. The shop where you could buy all your materials, rooms where students were at work in a wonderful smell of turpentine, others where they were drawing from the antique and studying anatomy and, across the road, the recreation rooms and the canteen. It was all very alarming and bewildering at first but a kind girl called Mary, whose parents knew my grandmother, guided my first faltering steps, and I loved being there from the first moment. I thought it was because I was doing what I liked doing best, but I now know it was also because the brilliant 'Toshie' had produced such an effective and harmonious place in which to work. The easels and donkeys and lighting and door furniture, and the student-proof finish on the stair walls, as well as the beautiful library, and the hen run, where one could retreat on sunny afternoons with an equally earnest companion to talk over life's problems, had all been thought out so well that it was a shame we took them so heedlessly for granted.

All students are, of course, expected to look peculiar as well as behaving crazily, and some succeed very well in maintaining this tradition. Some keep it up for a lifetime but that doesn't detract from the fact that in their art-school days they behaved exactly as they should have done.

In the summer of my first year there my parents took me to Stratford-on-Avon to see *Two Gentlemen of Verona* as a birthday treat. We queued in the late sunshine with the patient and predictable Shakespearean audience. A good sprinkling of dedicated, literary looking people among the family groups and foreign tourists, all very quiet and sedate. Just ahead of us, however, there was a group of young people providing enough noise and colour for all of us. They were laughing and singing and fooling about and enjoying themselves; about half a dozen of them in the most bizarre clothes –

though the long-haired boy in shorts and a green tunic laced with silver cord looked far more comfortable on a hot evening than I felt in my formal frock and silk stockings. Apart from him, it was hard to tell which were boys and which were girls, as my puzzled father remarked. But they were undoubtedly having fun and provided a pleasant contrast to all the decorum with their shaggy hair and colourful raiment.

As we inched forward and came nearer to them one of them turned and saw me and cried 'Why its RoseMARY!' (In England I am Rosem'ry and in Scotland I am, quite properly, Rose*mary*). They were my first-year mates from the School of Art, unrecognizably tanned and free after a summer in the sun. As I introduced them to my parents I took in their transformed appearance with awe and admiration. How sensible to have bare brown feet on such a hot day ('No,' said Davie, 'feet soon hardened and didn't notice gravel and stones') and what a nice change it made not to waste money on haircuts, and what fun to pile on the beads and hair ornaments willy-nilly, to such grand effect. It was as well we met because they had spent all their money on theatre tickets, as my father instantly guessed, so after the show we all had a most cheerful supper together and, well sustained, they went on their carefree way while we climbed into the car and drove home stimulated by the encounter.

In my first term I sat beside a pretty, blonde girl in a life class, and she became my best friend and remains so to this day. That particular class was taken by a pale, slight, nervous man to whom we were all merciless. I am deeply ashamed now remembering the drawings I did of him, which made the rest of the class fall about with laughter – and which I didn't hide when he came by. I think it never entered my head that he could be nervous of us. Why should he be? He was *old*, after all. Someone had said he was thirty-one, so he had had plenty of time to learn to be authoritative, for goodness' sake. But of course he hadn't learned and probably never would, and we all took full advantage, even though we did do some work. It has stood me in good stead, if with little help from him. It was not at all surprising, looking back, that he slid in and out of the class so seldom and so briefly, poor man.

The heating was particularly patchy in that room, and we could often watch the models develop blue or lavender hands and feet before the appointed rest time came. When it came they sat shivering on the radiators, eating oranges, and so returned to the model throne with bright pink bottoms. No doubt the heating is much improved now, but I am relieved to see so much still just as 'Toshie' planned the building to be. There was, of course, no Mackintosh cult in my student days (only a few isolated fans keeping the flag flying) and we took our surroundings totally for granted. His influence was everywhere, but we took that for granted too and regarded the rose and the lettering as a bit mannered and old-fashioned.

My best friend lived in Milngavie in a hospitable house with an excellent hard tennis court, her own sitting-room, and Annie in the kitchen producing endless teas and suppers for the group which foregathered at weekends. Once we had a stranger in our midst, a silent boy who said he was a good tennis player but had nowhere to play, so Louise asked him to come along on Saturday, at 3 p.m. He was a good player, and an asset, but on the court and off he was totally silent. He didn't seem to be shy, or overcome, just having nothing he wanted to say. He ate a large tea in amiable silence, and nodded with a pleased expression when someone offered him a lift back to Glasgow. He sat in the back between me and another girl, and suddenly he spoke. He said 'me knees is awful hot. It must be PAHssion' and then relapsed into silence again all the way into town.

Though student behaviour remains constant in essence, variations obviously occur with each era. Nowadays it is assumed that nobody of that age can get out of bed before 11 a.m., even if it is hoped that he or she will manage it now and then in term time. At the moment – and no doubt this phase will pass in a year or two – it is hard to know whether, even if ambulant, they are out of bed or not as they wander about, comatose, in the same sort of giant T-shirt they wear by day. My sister-in-law, when four Brazilian grandchildren were staying with her recently, had to ask the eldest, who was the only one who spoke anything but Portuguese, 'Is she dressed or not?' as she dealt out the cornflakes. Sometimes the answer was yes and sometimes no, but Belinda could never discern the distinction.

In our day, whatever our failings and misdemeanors, we turned up in time at the School of Art. We had to. There was a roll call, and you were in trouble if you were too often late. There were also marks for each subject, though nobody ever saw them, least of all the students. I only learned this last year when I was visiting the School of Art as a tourist, and stood for the third time in my life in the principal's room, admiring the splendid and well-planned Charles Rennie Mackintosh detail which I had been too frightened to notice on my first visit, as an applicant, or indeed on my second, two years later, when the then principal, W.O. Hutchinson, offered me a (eagerly accepted) job. The staff member who was showing us round mentioned the marking system, and when I said there had been no such thing in my day he said 'There was, you know. You just weren't told about it' and away he went to find the proof. He came back with a very small yellowing form, which reminded me of letters written by Dickens and Browning I had once read and which were all written on paper the size of playing cards.

On the tiny form, however, were recorded all my glorious marks. If *only* someone had told me. I am sure it would have changed, or at least much enhanced, my life. But in those far-off days self-esteem was not considered a virtue – it was far too close to that most despicable of sins, vanity – and lack of it never an excuse for bad behaviour as it is now, so authority felt it was doing its best for everyone in keeping the records secret.

There was, of course, a hierarchy in the School of Art, which was very right and proper. My friends and I were at the very bottom of the teeming heap, and at the apex were two or three brilliant painters in their last year. Lordly, heroic figures who could do, and did, exactly as they pleased. *We* knew what *they* looked like, though they, of course, wouldn't have known any of us from a bar of soap, and nor would we expect it. I was, therefore, astonished when one of them, one day, found me, addressed me by my name, and said Dan wanted to see me in the Rec at 11. 'What for?' I asked in dismay. 'He'll tell you' said the messenger in what seemed to me a sinister voice as he walked away. What had I done? *How* could I have transgressed enough to come to Dan's illustrious notice?

94

He was waiting for me in the Rec with coffee and chocolate digestives already on the table and my hand shook as I picked up my cup. Dan didn't notice as he had launched into a most unexpected speech. He had found God or, to be more exact, God had found him and he had responded. It had changed his whole life and this was all through a movement fashionable at the time called Moral Rearmament. Coming from a clerical household I had heard of this. I knew that they believed in testifying in public to one's sins and failings, and also, on a more positive note, in a daily 'Quiet Time' to allow God to make His wishes and hopes for this particular sinner known. The latter (more commonly known simply as prayer) could only be a good thing, and the former helpful, no doubt, to some, but to my questioning eye it seemed open to self-indulgence for those who craved attention. All the same I listened with unwavering attention and great interest to Dan's long and detailed description of his spiritual life, and how he had attained it, and how, with Divine guidance, he had spread the word through the School of Art. But now, he said, he was about to leave and carry on God's work elsewhere, and he had been for some time asking Him to name the person to take the precious baton from his hand.

'It wasn't until this morning that He told me' he said, his eyes shining with sheer joy 'and I could hardly wait to tell you.'

'Tell me what?' I said blankly.

95

'That it's you, of course. You are the one to carry on my work.'

'Me?' I squeaked. 'You don't *know* me.'

'God does' he said.

This was irrefutable. How had I got into this mad situation? How could I argue with God's word?

But there was no way, absolutely no way, that I would join Moral Rearmament, and I also felt that the lines between Dan and God had become crossed somewhere, because even if I agreed to 'carry on Dan's work' who would ever listen to mere me, following in his colourful footsteps? It took a very long and trying time to haul down his ebullient certainties. He was very, very disappointed in me and, indeed, aghast at my disregard of Divine instruction. In the end he became, understandably, extremely angry and, before he stalked off, banged the table till the coffee cups jumped, saying menacingly 'You – will – regret – this. You – will.'

But I never have, much as I hated to disappoint him so, and as time went on, felt increasingly thankful that I had resisted. Recently, looking at one of Dan's adult paintings in the Art Gallery – adequate, competent, enervating with its sad, sour, palette – it was hard to equate it with the glowing, passionate young man of that long-ago interview. He was true, however, to the age he was, with his talent and his ardour and his conviction, and he had played his part excellently in the continuous stream of the constant student. Single-minded, unreasoning, consumed with ideas they always are, always have been and, please God, always will be.

Miss Maguire

When I was seventeen, and had completed the course at the Glasgow School of Art, I went to London to get a job. It seemed to me most urgent that I should do this as soon as possible, since my family seemed to live in a permanent state of financial crisis, and the fact that I had, the year before, won a fashion-drawing competition in a national newspaper encouraged me to think that I could at least help a little.

Both my parents were hopeless at managing money, even though there wasn't much to manage, a clerical stipend not spreading far over the needs of a large family. My mother had been brought up with money, and my father hadn't, but neither, given their first cheque-books, had also been given any idea how cheque-books worked. She had her first one when she married at twenty, and was astonished, a few months later, to be summoned by a stern bank manager, with severe warnings about her first (but subsequently permanent) overdraft. She had thought a bell would ring when you ran out of money, and had no idea that the bank would honour cheques when your account was empty, and drive you into debt.

My father and his twin brother were in rather the same case. Young, handsome and lively, the twins set off for their first term at Oxford with new cheque-books, new freedom, and a new life which they enjoyed to the full. I don't know if my uncle was as profligate, but I know my father didn't pay off his shoe bill at Duckers till he was thirty.

My parents never learned, each feeling that the other was the extravagant one.

I have visions now of my mother, sitting up in bed in the first hours of the New Year (they were usually in bed by then but dutifully, at midnight, drank a toast to the New Year whereupon my father fell asleep at once and my mother applied herself to the 'New

Self' she was going to be from now on) and she had open on her knee a large account book with a burnt-orange linen cover.

It lasted, I think, all her life, because each page only took up one year. 'January 1st, 1925' read one page, the items petering out long before January had gone by, so 'January 1st, 1926' began just as hopefully on the next page. The long list of January pages, leading up to 1938, had made no dent in her optimism. She had a hopeful and romantic nature, and was the only person I have ever met whose first thought on waking was 'Oh what a lovely Wednesday morning. I wonder what nice thing will happen today'. She was handicapped in her accounts by not being able to trust her addition, so that was discouraging on both counts, not being sure if she had got it right and not liking the figure if she thought she had.

My father could add but couldn't be bothered. He thought there were far more important things to think about, and in this he was, of course, right, but it did lead us now and then into crisis. I remember one dramatic one when he decreed that he was going to lay up the car and cut off the telephone. So he did. He got about the parish on horseback (which is what he preferred anyway) and took no notice of my mother, going mad with frustration because she couldn't get anywhere except on foot.

The parishioners also became mad with frustration because of not being able to ring him up, so they clubbed together to re-install the telephone, and soon the car re-emerged, and we rollicked on until the next time. I am not at all sure where or how he managed to spend money, except that he was entirely open-handed, and would empty his pockets for anyone, when he could more prudently have referred them to a parish charity, but I remember one vivid example.

In the war Tony (my husband) and I were in London, as he was briefly at the War Office. We had rented a top-floor flat in Cadogan Gardens from a nice woman who was in a hurry to let, and to get away from bombs, so we got it very cheaply. We were both very young and unworldly, and so thought that her giant pink silk, gold-adorned bed in her lavishly mirrored bedroom was just sophisticated London ways. Even we understood it pretty rapidly when her hopeful callers kept climbing the long stairs to our door in the late evenings.

We were still living there – though we were soon to move out, feeling rather precarious when shrapnel from the defending guns in Hyde Park came through the ceiling on to our bed – when my father had to come to London for a meeting, and came to us for the night. My mother rang to say 'He's got enough for his train fare with him and nothing else. *Don't* let him spend any money. The bank manager is in a very fierce mood.' So we guarded him carefully, only releasing him in the morning to go to Sloane Square station, a short and straightforward walk with no tempting shops on the way, to get his train at Paddington. He got lost. He went by byways and, heaven alone knows how in that area, passed a saddler, and returned home bearing a magnificent new bridle. Unknown to my mother he had taken his cheque-book just in case.

So, one way and another, I had felt it was urgent that I should earn some money, and I got an extremely modest job drawing for an excellent – and subsequently very famous – couturier. My mother, worried about my living in London at such a tender age (what did she think I could do with a wage that barely covered my rent and food?) insisted that I should live in a hostel. When I first read Muriel Spark's *Girls of Slender Means* it was *déjà vu*, so exactly did it describe the hostel someone had recommended to her. The cheapest rooms were half-rooms, that is, a room divided up the middle by a partition which did not reach the ceiling. It seemed lunatic but I suppose it was the most cheese-paring solution.

So, I had a narrow cell with a good window on to the corner of Gloucester Road, and on the other side of the partition lived Miss Maguire. She was the light of my life during the six miserable months I spent in that job. I poured out my troubles to her at the end of each dreary day, and her warm sympathy tucked me in for the night like a duvet.

My job, which was to draw for the couturier because he could design but couldn't draw, would have been all right if I'd had enough drawing to do, but I didn't. I did other odd jobs about the place, and made friends with the house models, two tall good-looking girls, one dark and warm-hearted and coarse, one blonde and fastidious and fed-up, but in general I was neither fish, fowl, nor good red herring, and in the long periods of having no drawing to do I wasn't even learning any new or useful skills.

So it was depressing. As was returning at the end of the long day to the dreary hostel – or would have been had it not been for Miss Maguire. During the day I thought of her often, looking foward to all I would tell her that night, how I would twist the dismal incidents and make them sound funny, and she would respond with peals of light, girlish laughter.

And she never failed me. Her ready laughter buoyed up my downcast spirits, and I felt myself an individual again in the light of her unflagging interest in me. We exchanged our lives (though I hadn't much to tell) over the partition in the long sad evenings which only led to another dreadful day for us both. Miss Maguire became for me, home. Comfort and affection and concern, all the home things I missed so acutely, were contained in her enchanting golden voice.

I only saw her once, and that was near the end of my time in the hostel. I could, of course, have seen her at any time but it just didn't happen and I was too fond of her disembodied voice to bring it about deliberately. I was sorry when I had seen her. I knew, roughly, what her age must be, but my imagination had built up a very different picture of her appearance. Her voice was so light, so singing, so up-and-down and gay, that I thought she would be a little, lightly built, blonde, perhaps a trifle faded now – I knew she had been forty-two when her father had died over two years ago – and dressed in the good tweeds she had always worn at home in Ireland and with her father's signet ring on her small, delicate hand.

I knew every room of her house in Ireland after I had known her for a few weeks. She had always lived there, and as her mother had died in childbirth she and her father and two old servants had had it contentedly to themselves. I soon felt as if I, too, had played tennis in the spongy grass court by the stables, and driven in the old, grey Austin down the bumpy drive to exactly similar tennis parties in other local houses. The sound of old Mary drawing back the long, faded curtains in the blue room and letting in the morning sun was so familiar to me that I felt it was I, and not Miss

Maguire, who had been thus awakened in the big mahogany bed. I knew about the tray of china tea and whisky that appeared every evening sharp at 9.30. The cups were blue and gold Crown Derby and the whisky came in a silver-mounted eighteenth-century decanter, and, as she put the tray down, old Mary always said 'There now. Something nice for each of ye.' I looked back, with Miss Maguire, on the view of the blue hills beyond the lawns, the copper beech by the gate and, in the spring the scyllas and primroses and grape hyacinths growing in the bed outside the drawing-room window.

I felt as if I had seen for myself the affectionate companionship between Miss Maguire and her father, and I knew in my own heart her grief when he died, leaving a bleak trail of debts, so there was nothing to be done but sell up and come to London. She came because she couldn't bear to stay alone in Ireland, and she must get a job, and for that she must have some training. The skills she had were not much use when it came to earning a living. She couldn't cook or wash or iron. She could only organize two old servants who needed no organizing at all, and be a cheerful and pleasant companion and hostess. The latter talent had not, however, been called into use for some years past – her father had become old and frail and wanted no company but hers and she was happy, living quietly with him against the familiar background, the beloved child, not counting the cost, not looking ahead.

When it was explained to her that she must now earn her living the only solution she could see was a secretarial college, and in those days typing and shorthand were the only essential qualifications. She had just enough money for a year's course there and at the end of that time – so they told her, not knowing her – she would be equipped with skills sufficient to earn a large and easy salary. Indeed, to choose her employer. An MP would be nice, she thought sometimes, near the hub of things. Or an author – she would not mind if he were temperamental and difficult; dear father had often needed a great deal of love and understanding. She thought a great deal about the pleasant job ahead of her so that she would not concentrate too much on her unhappy present.

She was in the middle of her second term when I arrived at the hostel, and her indomitable spirit tried at first to disguise from me her tortured days at the college, but as we became friends I learned to discern the truth behind her gallant words.

Her classmates ignored her, giggling across her, sharing the sort of talk she had never known because she had had no girlfriends when she was young in the remote Irish house, needing no-one but her father. She *couldn't* get shorthand into her head, while the others, fresh from school, absorbed it and swept past her contemptuously. She did her homework faithfully, but it meant nothing when it was done just as it had meant nothing in the first place. She repeated rules and phrases over and over and over, trying to learn them by heart, but she had never known how to learn, and her heart was filled with alarm and loneliness.

She never said a self-pitying word to me, but I knew how it was. I knew her so well by now. Listening to her musical voice, doggedly cheerful at the end of another terrible day, my heart ached for her. As we talked I could, in my mind, see her sitting on her narrow bed 3 feet away, the frail faded blonde, the good shabby tweeds, dear father's ring. . . .

I was right about the ring. All the same, I regarded it, when at last we met by chance in the hostel's dining-room, without recognition. We were sitting at the same table and I was shocked when she made some remark about the dismal hostel food. I stared at her, at first unable to believe that the familiar golden voice had emerged from such an unlikely exterior.

I had been right in nothing except father's ring, dark and square on her plump pink hand. Her face matched her hand, pinkly soft, marshmallow soft, and brightly pink where she had been heavy-handed with the blusher. Her hair was a bright, unlikely gold, in masses of little curls piled improbably upwards, and down in a coy and curling fringe. Her eyes were round and bewildered and blue, the skin around them gently crumpled. Her whole soft billowing body was clad in pink and blue and little frills, secured now and then with one of her mother's less-good brooches (the good ones had had to go, I knew, with the house and furniture and old grey Austin).

She was delighted to see me and said I was *much* prettier than she had imagined. I choked in the effort to say the same sort of thing to her. 'I never thought', she cried happily, 'that I would have a *real* friend on the other side of that dreadful partition. When the housekeeper first showed me that *tiny* room, about the size of the bathroom at home, and I knew I was to live in just *one half* of it, I nearly wept! It wasn't just being so squashed – and I *am* squashed you know darling, because of my few bits and pieces from home – but I thought how terrible it would be to have someone on the other side of the partition listening to me brushing my teeth and turning the pages of my book, and imagining I don't know *what*. But with you, darling it's so different. I just count the minutes until I hear you come in.' So long as I listened and didn't look at her I could answer normally, but the rest of the meal was a strain. I could hardly wait until we were back in our own cubicles and could talk over the partition as we usually did, and Miss Maguire's bright cheeks and over-flowing pink and blue bosom would be hidden from view.

My relief when she regained invisibility was doubled that evening because, at the dinner table, she had tried to tell me more about Mr Winthrop. He was the teacher at her shorthand class and must have had more imagination than Miss Bell, who instructed in typing, because all this term he had been conspicuously patient with Miss Maguire, and gradually the shorthand days lost, for her, the nightmare qualities which the typing days still held in full measure under Miss Bell's bewildering speed and cutting tongue.

Miss Maguire talked more and more about Mr Winthrop. Soon, I could see, she was endowing him in her mind with all the noble characteristics her father appeared to have had and for which she had sought, in vain, in a prospective husband. 'I never met a man, you know, darling,' she would sigh, 'who could compare with father. I did indeed want to be a wife and have little children of my own, but father set me too high a standard in men. Although,' she added, a coy note creeping into her voice 'I've had plenty of chances, of course.' 'Of *course*' I agreed enthusiastically.

She said slowly and thoughtfully 'Would you say – of course I know you are very young and maybe not much experienced in life, but you are *very* sensible – would you say that a girl of my age would have to give up thought of marriage now? I mean, it is possible, is it not, that there are men – older men – just looking for a wife who is more mature than those silly little girls at the college?' 'Oh yes, certainly there are' I said, knowing nothing about it but anxious to banish the wistfulness from her voice. 'How would you suggest would be a good way to meet such a man? I mean, taking into consideration the fact that I know so few people in England – not enough to reckon on meeting him in the normal way, in someone's drawing-room?' I felt exceedingly anxious. It seemed to me terrible that anyone of Miss Maguire's age should believe in this forlorn hope to the extent of being prepared to act on it. She would, I was convinced, be hideously disappointed either gradually and sadly or by a shattering blow. It would be better if she concentrated on her secretarial course, however hard she found it.

So, inadvertently and disastrously, I encouraged her to talk about Mr Winthrop, which she so clearly loved to do, as I thought one could safely count him out of the husband hunt. She had described him as '*very* good-looking, dark with wonderful eyes and hands. Rather slight, about twenty-seven or twenty-eight, but perhaps he is more. . . .' At first she spoke of him in an entirely maternal tone and I, in my youthful assurance that these were the only feelings a woman of her age could decently entertain for a man of his, never noticed when the maternal note in her voice was replaced by a very different one.

Looking back on it, I remember all sorts of things I didn't notice at the time. I missed nothing by not being at those shorthand classes.

Miss Maguire told me every single thing that was said and thought and felt throughout. I remember when jealousy began to prick her if Mr Winthrop praised another student ('the silly simpering girl always showing off') and if Mr Winthrop criticized someone Miss Maguire was delighted ('she deserved it. She does nothing but play around. I could feel he was *really* angry with her but of course he didn't say much. He has such beautiful manners – that reminds me so much of father').

Mr Winthrop never criticized Miss Maguire's work, nor did he praise her. I think he must have regarded her simply as his cross, and because he was a kind young man, recognized her gallantry in attempting the Herculean task she showed no sign of mastering. But she took this absence of praise or blame as a sign that he had 'a special feeling' for her. I felt cold with horror when she said this. What was she imagining now for heaven's sake? From that moment I recognized Mr Winthrop as a danger, a menace, but by then it was too late for me to protect her. I could only listen every evening to accounts of his words, his actions, his appearance, and live with Miss Maguire – and nearly as tense as she was though from different motives – for the dawn of Monday, Wednesday and Friday when for two hours she would sit in the same room with him.

Miss Maguire's chief enemy in the class was a girl called Liz Morris. One day she had overheard herself being spoken of 'most insultingly and ridiculously' in the cloakroom by Liz, and had never forgiven her. I had not forgiven her either. I didn't know what Liz had said because Miss Maguire was too upset to tell me just what it was, but when I heard my friend's defiant scorn break down in tears of humiliation, I hated Liz with a deadly venom. I threw a bar of milk chocolate over the partition to Miss Maguire to console her, but there was little else I could do but go on hating Liz. Which I did. Miss Maguire and I spent many satisfactory evenings after that, hating her together, and despising her wild red hair and the emptiness of her foolishly pretty face. Also the gangs of young men competing to escort her home from the college, Miss Maguire saying darkly that she was sure they 'got what they wanted all right'. We hugged ourselves with glee when Mr Winthrop ticked Liz off in class, which he frequently did, appearing to share our feelings to the full, and to dislike Liz more every week.

As the bright spring days went on Miss Maguire became more and more light-hearted and happy on Mondays, Wednesdays and Fridays (though shorthand still eluded her) until one day her cup overflowed and she and Mr Winthrop lunched at the same table in the college canteen. Usually he lunched out, understandably eager to escape the college environment as soon as possible, so she was surprised to see him there. He came in late, and the canteen was crowded. All the chairs were taken except the other one at Miss Maguire's table, because nobody ever came and sat with her if they could help it. They must have been a pitiless lot, those students, and many of them undoubtedly followed the high spirits and flaming red hair of the mocking Liz Morris.

'I just looked up from my book, darling,' she said, her voice liquid with joy, 'and there he was, just standing there and saying "is this chair taken, Miss Maguire?" And oh, darling, what a lunch we had! What a perfect gentleman he is! It was as though a stream of *complete* sympathy flowed between us. He felt it too. I knew he must, but at the end he said "It's been nice getting to know you a bit, Miss Maguire". Just quietly with a smile – just like that. "It's been nice getting to know you a bit, Miss Maguire" . . . Wasn't that charming?' I couldn't see where all this was going to end, but I was certain of disaster. Sometimes I almost believed in Miss Maguire's secret hopes, so infectious was her own happiness, and so vivid her imagination. And then solemn common sense would rise in me again, and I knew on how precarious a foundation she had built her tottering edifice.

On Friday she was always home before me, and I heard her welcoming 'That you, darling? How did it go today?' as soon as I opened the door. But one Friday at the end of the day I came home very late, cross and tired. I'd had a long frustrating day doing tedious little jobs and no drawing, and then at 5 o'clock in rushed the boss with sheaves of designs for a country wedding, which all had to be drawn – bride, bride's mother, going-away suit, bridesmaids and pages – for the late post. I was going to relieve my feelings by telling

Miss Maguire how awful I felt, tired, and hungry too because of course I'd missed supper.

I opened my door on silence, which was most disconcerting. I sighed. I missed her acutely and was longing to let off steam. I took off my jacket and, squeezing between the end of the bed and the dressing-table, stuffed it into the narrow cupboard. Exhausted as I was, I felt too restless to prepare for bed, so I picked up a book and sat down on my bed to read. In the silence I heard a small sound, like a gasp, from Miss Maguire's side of the partition. Or thought I did. I listened, decided I had imagined it, and returned to my book.

Then I heard it again. Could she be there, after all, perhaps asleep? I said uncertainly 'Are you there, Miss Maguire?' feeling foolish because I was certain she wasn't. I jumped, startled, when her voice, muffled and broken, answered 'Yes, darling, I am'.

'Oh, Miss Maguire, what is wrong?' I cried, longing to help, but somehow it never entered my head to go next door and see what I could do. We kept each other's privacy with extra care because we had so little. She was sobbing now, unrestrainedly, and I realized she must have been crying before I came in, and stopped for my sake. 'I'm just a silly old woman' she kept saying and I was appalled, never having heard her refer to herself as anything but 'a girl' before. She cried and cried, and I did what I could from my side of the wall, playing the *Prelude à L'après-midi d'une Faune* very softly on my portable gramophone, because it was her favourite, and throwing over to her my birthday bottle of scent. I don't think I did much good – I think she just cried herself out – but at last she stopped and in a dull dreary voice began to tell me what had happened.

'It was a beautiful class today and Mr Winthrop was so kind, so very kind, to me. I was sure he was remembering our lunch and I was hoping – oh so hoping – that we might lunch together again. Then in the canteen I thought I would faint from pleasure when he came in, just as I dreamed, and came to my table again, just as before . . . Our lunch began as it did before, so friendly, so *sympathetic* . . . Oh I was so happy. We both had the shepherd's pie and we talked so freely, so easily, that the time just flew. He said he would get my pudding for me and was just about to get up and join the queue when I looked up and saw Liz Morris standing there, bold as brass. He saw her at the same time and he said – he said "Hullo, torment" . . .'. Miss Maguire's voice faltered and she paused, and then she went on in the same grey level tone, 'He said "Hullo, torment – sit down. Have half my chair" and she sat down, and he looked across at me and he said "I don't think it matters telling *you*, Miss Maguire, though I wouldn't want anyone else to know, but Liz and I have a secret. We've had an awful job keeping it from all these people here because if they knew our lives wouldn't be worth a moment's purchase, and Liz has still got her finals to pass, but you'll keep it under your hat, won't you? How we've managed to keep it dark for a year I simply can't think, but by this time next month this lazy little good-for-nothing will be my wife."'

Lustreless London rain had begun to fall outside the oblong of my window in a dispirited way. It was falling on the wet, grey street, on the cars hurrying home, the umbrellas hurrying along the pavement, and the buses whining to a stop at the traffic lights and grinding forward when the light became green. Inside our little divided room Miss Maguire and I stared in horror at the trampled remains of her dignity, her dreams, and her heart. Frantically I searched my mind for hope, for her, for myself . . . Perhaps, I thought, her kind, good, foolishness will heal her. She won't be able to sustain hatred. She won't be able to bear the memory of truth. In time it will seem she was the honoured confidante of this romantic pair. Damn them and curse them. Damn them and curse them. I rose abruptly and pulled the flimsy curtains across the quiet callous rain with such savagery that one of them tore, and the triangular hole hung there, black and resentful, flapping at me.

A Winning Streak

I can't imagine why I have this vision of myself at heaven's gate, asking St Peter not only to let me in but also to redesign me in so many areas. Not just to make me small and blonde (to which he would doubtless reply that he was not interested in vanity redesigning), but to fill in all those yawning gaps in proper or sensible function which I can identify but somehow can't repair. Of course he would say, and rightly, 'Why do you suppose you qualify for entry at all, with or without so much rectification?' It would indeed be hard to know where to start.

I have always loved the inspiring phrase 'a winning streak' visualizing a bright gold lightning-shaped zig-zag shooting through someone's body, almost visible to the admiring onlooker, but I not only haven't a thread of such a thing in me, rather a hollow pale-grey void. One of the most tiresome handicaps under which I labour is not being able to care who wins – though I eagerly applaud those who do – and am therefore unable to play any game with any sense. Some games are fascinating – I can recognize that. And some are great fun to play, like tennis, which I really, really enjoyed even though I always had a problem remembering whose side I was on, even when playing singles. Knowing my limitations all too well – I had a reliable service and now and then a splendid forehand drive and nothing else at all to offer, in addition to this absent-minded attitude about winning and losing – I enjoyed home tennis on our bumpy grass court with not enough run-back at one end.

David and Haro and Joan and I played – whenever the court was dry enough – constantly and casually, whatever we happened to be wearing, sweaters or jodhpurs or bathing pants, and bare feet if we were too lazy to fetch rubber-soled shoes, and I never remember any acrimonious games. This would be understandable if the other three had my particular affliction, but they hadn't. They played properly

109

and well. In fact Haro and Joan, the two youngest, were some sort of under-twelve champions in their under-twelve day. All through our adolescence we played this sort of tennis at home, much enhanced one summer when David bought a record of *Eine Kleine Nachtmusik* which he played, with a loud needle, on the portable gramophone set down by the net post to encourage us while we banged the balls back and forth.

It was all very different when our father now and then decided to join us. For him tennis and all games, were of passionate intensity. He was a winning streak personified. He had just missed his tennis Blue at Oxford (but had a long-distance running one to console him) and every time he played had to change into tennis kit, even for half an hour if that was all the time he had, and play with new or, at least newish, balls. A sacred box of half a dozen was kept in the oak settle in the hall, and woe betide any of us who went on playing with them after he had left us, and lost one in the lilac bushes, or left them out in the rain. We used any old balls, khaki with age and half bald, and found his six pure ones, lightly stained with lime-green grass patches, quite disconcerting but rather fun after a bit, so we were often tempted to transgress. He was a kind and indulgent father in real life, but not on court, so I formed the idea that seriously good players were all devoid of tolerance or politeness.

When I presently married another seriously good player I was *amazed*. He showed no sign of wanting to kill me (or any other inadequate partner) when I did something foolish, and if we lost, we lost, and it didn't matter because it was only a game. (If anyone had used the words 'only a game' to my father he would have made no sense whatsoever of the phrase.)

One summer all four of us entered the well-respected tennis tournament held in the local town. It was graced by the occasional Wimbledon player, and in the junior section were those who would, in time, qualify for this accolade. (It was, of course, long before the days of children training, with dedicated ferocity, towards this end at the expense of the rest of their lives.) I can't imagine how I scraped in but needless to say I lasted only one round. One agonizing round. I remember with still vivid horror the packed stands all round the court while I scampered about, terrified, and muttering 'I'm supposed to *win*. I've got to *win*' to myself like a mantra, and a fat lot of good it did. The words were meaningless to me then as they are now. Except on this occasion (when I was scared witless) I enjoyed playing, on an entirely physical level. I liked hitting a good shot, or placing a ball just where I wanted, or outwitting someone on the other side of the net. Though, as to the last, they could just as well have been my side of the net. It was only making a point in an argument, after all . . .

For me, the pleasure of playing was exactly the same as swimming in a warm Greek sea – just physical enjoyment with nothing else in my head. That, of course, is not how one plays games properly, and my siblings, tennis partners and my husband, have been very forbearing. Though tennis parties were usually fun, with a pot luck of people and standards, club tennis is another matter.

I have only experienced two clubs, one in Sri Lanka (and so long ago that it was Ceylon) and one in the Home Counties. The latter club was, for me, horrible. Everyone wanted badly to win. Everyone was extremely serious about it, which is of course a very proper attitude.

My husband Tony, enclosed in a London office all the long week, was delighted to be able to spend all his summer Saturday afternoons playing tennis until the light failed and I was glad he could. Luckily for me I seldom played, as I had an excellent excuse in the shape of three young children on the side-lines, and so we amused ourselves as best we could until it was time for me to help with the teas and as soon after that as we decently could we departed for home. 'Those children surely don't go to bed as early as this?' I heard someone say testily as we left one Saturday. We all overheard and looked at each other and laughed.

The other was when I was seventeen. My uncle was the government agent in Kandy, living in the Old Palace, which is now a museum, and I used the £100 my paternal grandmother had left me to go out to stay there for a few months. It was a well-spent £100. Not only did I experience the last days of the Raj, but the extraordinary life lived by the ex-pat society there. With rare exceptions, there were no old people and no children. My cousins, my contemporaries, had seen very little of their parents since they were seven years old, having been sent home to school and then having only very rare visits from their mother, and to some children their father was unknown until their schooling was over.

There were lots of young men there, working in the colonial civil service and on the tea estates and elsewhere, and not nearly enough girls, so any new girl was an event and couldn't fail to have a heady time, and so I did. There, the tennis club was a daily event, and between tea and dinner everyone foregathered on the excellent courts, with 'peons' to act as ball boys, and a lot forgiven you just because you were that precious and rare commodity, a girl. Not, of course, by Uncle Tom. Extremely nice and kind to me in ordinary life, he was just like my father, and his other five brothers when it came to games. I soon learned to lurk in the pavilion when fours were being arranged lest I should find myself playing against – or worse, with – Uncle Tom. Fortunately, owing to the shortage of girls, there were always several young men lurking with me, anxious to partner me and to help protect me from my own follies.

It was in Ceylon that I learned about bridge. Not how to play it (to try and teach me would have been an uphill task for a saint) but about it. My parents never played, and by chance I had never encountered it before. Uncle Tom and Aunt May were keen, and when they had one of their frequent bridge evenings I would be sitting reading at the other end of the long room. It was an odd room, with almost life-size figures in low relief, white on grey, all round the walls, and as it was just across the road from the Temple of the Tooth there was the pleasure of watching from the window, twice a day, the sacred elephants going by. I can remember now with delight the soft 'ploof' sound of their feet upon the road, gentle and dignified. I had tried going back to my room to read during the bridge parties, much alarmed by the tension and acrimony which seemed concomitant to them, but Aunt May pointed out that though I hadn't meant to seem rude, it looked rude to slither away, so thereafter I stayed. And learned. I am sure they were only normal bridge fours but to me they were unbelievable, with all the arguing and derision and despair.

This was meant to be *fun*? This was played for *pleasure*? Uncle Tom played as he played tennis – well, focused on winning, intemperate with slowness or folly, and speaking his mind. Aunt May, slow and smiling and not raising her voice, spoke hers, and so, in various manner, did the guests. Calm didn't descend when the guests had gone, as my uncle and aunt held an angry and detailed post mortem. If the bridge party had been a pre-dinner session, this meant that dinner was uncomfortable, and the curry tasted like ashes to me, though Uncle Tom would send messages to the kitchen via Daniel, who waited on us, to say it wasn't nearly hot enough.

Though I can't regret not being able to play bridge, or indeed, any other sensible card game, it has been a handicap when it came to playing cards with small children, even though their games are at about my level. Many is the time I have been accused by a three or four-year-old 'You aren't *concentrating*' and 'You didn't *think*'. Too right. I wasn't and didn't, and I was ashamed. Quite apart from being an irritating opponent when I was supposed to be giving them some fun or entertainment, it is paltry not to be able to keep my mind on such a simple task for half an hour.

It became rather solemn when we acquired children of our own, and I could consider the maternal traits I would rather they didn't inherit. Fairly high on the long list was this one, because it is so stupid, but I was at a loss to know what to do about it except let events take their course. I couldn't have pretended, because not only would I not know how to keep it up, but I wouldn't have fooled three intelligent, perceptive children for a moment. I just had to hang on to the hope that they would ignore me and follow their father's example, that of a good and efficient games and sports player who recognized games for what they were, just games.

Shopping

The constant threats of a future dominated by shopping by TV or Internet seem to sidle by the point of it all. Shopping is not, even now, only about acquiring goods and paying for them, though admittedly this idea seems more and more prevalent, at least in theory.

In practice, of course, it leaves out the human element. Cooks, for a start, prefer to meet their avocados and carrots and cabbages face to face, and few people would choose a suit without seeing and feeling the cloth, though the ease and rise of mail order, and returning what you don't like, means you can do all that from home very well. We owe a lot to the American firms in this area, as they brought to our shores the novel idea of staffing their telephones with human beings, and amiable ones at that, which makes telephone shopping easy and pleasant. The system is a life-saver to many of us who live a distance from shops, or are cut for time, or can't get out, or all three.

This is an extension of the system my mother used endlessly. She sent off to well-known London shops for this or that 'on approval'. Though she had no account at that particular shop, a large dress box duly trustingly arrived, for whatever it was to be tried on and eventually paid for, if kept, and if not it went back, and that was that. Were people much more honourable in those days? The shops can't have lost much by the 'on approval' system or they wouldn't have continued it, but it was very like the present mail order minus the credit cards.

Looking even further back, my grandmother's shopping seemed very orderly and peaceful. All, except for Burberrys for one and all, and fabrics from Liberty's for dresses and cushion covers, was done in the familiar Glasgow shops. Sauchiehall Street was then full of high quality shops, and though she lived near by, her day usually began by telephoning this or that shop with her order and accompanied by a long, cosy, chat. 'Oh *hello*, Mrs Hedderwick', said the voice from the greengrocer at Charing Cross. 'How are *you*? Wait and I'll get Mr Mackenzie for you.' Then an equally warm but masculine voice took over 'Now Mrs Hedderwick, I was just that minute thinking about you. I've got some lovely muscat grapes in and I know you like them.' 'Oh that *is* nice', said Granny, 'and I have a long list here, but first tell me about your Ian. Did he get his university place? He did? Oh *isn't* that good. You and Mrs Mackenzie must be *so* proud of him . . . Oh, I know . . . it seems no time at all . . . That is most excellent news – do congratulate him most warmly from me' and then she embarked on her list.

Often she shopped in person, driven in the huge stuffy Daimler by the sour, dour, chauffeur, Wilson, and often taking grandchildren with her. I found these expeditions fascinating, especially the elegant and spacious grocer's Cooper's, where Granny sat perched by the counter on a little bentwood chair (she never once sat back in her chair, having been taught at Cheltenham Ladies College that ladies never did) and discussed teas and coffees and butter and bacon and oatcakes. Behind the counter white-coated men sliced the chosen butter off a huge block, and swiftly patted it into a perfect, patterned, rectangle, enclosed in a neat, grease-proof paper packet. Others slid giant silver discs across ham and bacon, cutting it to customer's orders, or dealt sugar into stiff, blue paper bags. Granny didn't buy any of the biscuits which were on display in huge glass-fronted tins. Shop biscuits, except chocolate ones, were rather looked down on, and therefore a great treat to us children. And doubtless, even as Granny shopped, Kate the cook was at work in the long, clinically clean kitchen at Clairmont Gardens making shortbread, and Grasmere gingerbread, and the square water-biscuits Grandad was so fond of, with baked-in bubbles.

With luck we would go from Cooper's to Reid and Todd, to buy yet more of the black leather loose-leaf notebooks with India-paper pages which Granny used by the score. She had all sizes, and each one was dedicated to one or another of her activities and charities and committees. Her handbag was full of them. One could hardly lift it off the floor. At least one notebook was extracted at every mealtime, to lie open beside her place at table, so that she could jot down items as she remembered them to be dealt with for the Scottish

Mother's Union (of which she was President), Dorcas, the church, the Scottish Orchestra, various people who needed her help, others whose help she must enlist, and no doubt shopping lists as well.

Clothes, by the time she was elderly and I was shopping with her came all from Madame Murielle's small scented shop. Madame Murielle, with her soft Glaswegian voice and huge moist teapot-brown-eyes rather alarmed me, and always made my kilt and Fair Isle jersey feel very hot and tickly. But Granny, who loved clothes, was very happy there, as Madame Murielle helped her choose dresses and exquisite pastel-coloured georgette blouses, and neat little black suits and fashionable hats.

I was born too late for the massive annual organization involved in moving into a rented country house for four months in the summer. The house was near enough Glasgow for the men to commute to the office or practice, and large enough to accommodate all the friends and relations my grandparents were eager to invite. As there were no shops near by everything was ordered daily from Glasgow and came down to Thankerton by train.

When Granny died at ninety-two, some of the unused summer order forms were found, and they said

From   Mrs J.D. Hedderwick
                 East End
                 Thankerton

Please send the following, addressed as above, and put in the Peebles van on the 4.20 p.m. train from Central Station.' (Her ordinary headed writing paper was ordered by the ream, in two sizes and 800 envelopes for each size.)

The order for the newsagent was also found, catering for all ages and tastes: 'The *Glasgow Herald*, the *Statesman*, the *London Daily News*, the *Daily Graphic*, the *Sphere*, *Punch*, *Illustrated London News*, *Black & White*, *British Weekly*, *Weekly Times*, the *Churchman*, the *Signal*, *Good Words*, *Little Folks*, the *Children's Friend* and *Tiny Tots*'.

Lavish days indeed. No wonder all the friends and relations came so eagerly for their holidays. There was also a note on the actual migration in June 1900.

Three lorries at 6 p.m. on Tuesday to load up.
Lorries leave on Wednesday 6 a.m.
Five men 1/6 each.

In addition to all the kitchen supplies, which took up a lot of room (flour and oatmeal and sugar were bought by the sack) there had to be everybody's clothes for four months, and all the surface contents of the drawing-room, so that everyone would feel at home, albeit in someone else's house. So in went the rose-silk cushions and the ivory paper knife made out of an elephant's tusk that was too big to be of use, and the books that lay about and were never read, and piles of music, since everyone was expected to sing or play, and the silver box for sweeties and the ornamental brass scissors that didn't cut very well and the blotter and ink-stand and pen-tray.

Once at East End, all the alien cushions and pictures and so forth were stowed away, so that by the time the family arrived it was all

Our grandparents, with Nan and Gaickie in the centre and Granny's sisters, Jessie and Rosie, on the left.

very home-like, with the rose-coloured silk cushions and the unread books and the brass scissors that wouldn't cut and all the rest of it. In addition the lorries were laden with golf clubs and tennis rackets and bow and arrows (there was an excellent archery walk, and Granny was very skilled at this) and rods and guns and also high-chairs and prams if any small children were present or expected. Granny, a born organizer, kept copious notes and the whole thing ran on oiled wheels.

My mother loved shopping, but until she was over forty did little or no house-hold shopping because she couldn't cook and therefore said she didn't know what to buy. She behaved like a memsahib, delegating this chore, and, like many a memsahib, was thoroughly exploited as a penance for evading her duty in this field. She had scorned, as a girl, to follow her sister's example and take a cookery course at the Glasgow 'DO' School, and her mother had only ever entered a kitchen to order the day's meals, so it was easy to avoid a task she felt she wouldn't do well. She didn't like not doing things well, so was not prepared to try her hand. This was bad luck on all the family as we couldn't afford a real cook, and therefore had anyone who could be persuaded to come and have a shot at it for some meagre wage, and we ate the most appalling food as a result, even by the dreary standards of the day.

One of these semi-cooks had once been briefly in service as a kitchen maid, and had learned to cook 'Kromeskies' there. Or not exactly learned. I have never discovered what 'Kromeskies' are supposed to be like, but it is a fair bet that they are not supposed to have uncooked bacon wrapped round some substance inside a pale flaccid, greasily fried coating. I can write with feeling as we had these things day in and day out, and even when hungry we found them unwelcome to say the least. Fortunately a village lad courted, and then swept off, the 'Kromeskie'-maker, and we then had Flora, whose mental balance was precarious and much affected by phases of the moon, and so therefore was our food.

Lunch came in late one day. Cold ham, and some lettuce on a saucer (there were six of us gathered hungrily round the table) and then a huge dish under a seldom-used silver dome. When my mother lifted this off it disclosed one boiled potato. '*One* potato, Flora?' she said questioningly. 'Divide it', said Flora and bolted from the room.

When, in the war, the supply of quasi-cooks ran out, my mother had no choice but to screw up her courage and cook. Of course, since she liked good food, she was soon cooking excellently and went on to enjoy it thoroughly and look back on the wasted years with regret.

Then she entered the butcher's shop and the baker's and grocer's and greengrocer's and she enjoyed that, even in the sparsely stocked and severely rationed wartime shops, because they extended the range of her favourite places beyond clothes and shoe shops, and bookshops and antique dealers, and she made friends in all the shops. Few people can have learned the art of cooking in harder circumstances. Not only with severe rationing and shortages of all kinds, including fuel, but in a teeming and fluctuating household. Family and friends came on leave, bringing friends, some with ration books and some not. A sister-in-law, plus children, sought refuge from London bombs. Granny and her faithful Edith were there permanently, and so was a wounded brother convalescing, and so, soon, was I (Tony having been posted to India), with a beautiful, blonde baby. My mother fed all comers, and contrived and expanded meals from minimal ingredients, and it is good to reflect on the fact that she did, in the end (though it took an unconscionable time) see the return of well-stocked shops and plenty of ingredients for the cooking in which she by now took pride.

Because she took such delight in shopping and could find a shop in the least likely place, or treasures behind a forbidding façade, it was fun to shop with her. Apart, that is, for shoe shops, whence to accompany her was a penance. She would conceive the idea of a certain pair of shoes and *must* have them. So off we would go, 20 miles to Cheltenham, to begin the hunt.

On one of these occasions, in an up-market shoe shop, she was being looked after by a most patient and painstaking young man. With twenty-two pairs of shoes all scattered around her because she wouldn't let him put any away just in case one pair would turn into just what she wanted, he had vanished to find the twenty-third pair.

He was away a very long time, and presently she said 'Where can he be? What on earth can he be doing?'

'He has gone', I said tersely, 'to have a good cry before returning to the fray.' She did laugh, but slightly shame-facedly and when the poor man returned she looked anxiously at his downy cheeks for signs of tears, and quickly decided on one of the pairs she had already tried on and rejected.

They weren't right, of course. Once home, they became one of the mistake-buys, mourned as a trick of fate, and nothing to do with her. Still, she had loved the expedition and all that time in the shop, so it was cheap at the price for her, and I do hope the young man went home exceedingly proud of himself, although he must have been completely exhausted.

Since my mother couldn't cook when I was married, nor could I, and I, too, had to learn from scratch in various flats and lodgings all around the country, and the rations were incredibly small. There were kind people in the shops, however, in all the strange towns and villages as I followed the drum for the year Tony remained in this country. Helpful butchers who recognized a very young and ignorant customer when they saw one, and advised on how best to deal with the week's meat ration for two, a horrid little gristly lump the size of a tennis ball. There were kind neighbours giving me hints on how to be a frugal housewife. 'When you make a shopping list, put down everything you need, and then cross off everything you *could* do without.' And 'Don't rinse out the milk bottle as soon as you have poured the milk into a jug. Leave it for a moment. There's another teaspoonful there.'

The problems of cooking with little food and often no fuel – in one bitter postwar winter we were living in an all-electric house, and the electricity was turned off every day from 10 until 4 – was compounded by there being nothing to cook in. I had two very beaten-up old saucepans from kind friends who could spare them, and a discarded frying pan from home with an undulating base, and that was all until I had been married six years. I could bake things in the few welcome Pyrex dishes we'd been given as wedding presents in 1941 and I had two large green-edged, cream enamel plates which I had found in a village shop and bought because I thought they looked so forbidding that they might be useful. The woman behind the counter said 'That's a *good* buy, dear. Always useful, these are.' I couldn't imagine how at the time, but I soon found out. They were all right in the oven for baking, and if I had a gas cooker at the time, served as rather precarious pans for delicacies like dried-egg scrambled egg which, whatever one did to it, tasted like shoe-polish. I have the hideous great plates still. A bit chipped but still in use. That shop woman was quite right. I baked my first-ever cake in a cocoa tin someone gave me, because of course there were no cake tins either.

At one point during the war there had been an appeal for metal 'to make Spitfires' (which we learned much later was an entirely pointless exercise supposed to raise national morale by involving people on a personal level). So towns sent their railings – and therefore could no longer patriotically grow potatoes and cabbages in the park flower beds because they had no protection – and stately homes sent their splendid gates, and housewives sent their saucepans and roasting tins. My mother-in-law, nothing if not patriotic, sent her son's precious and extensive Hornby 00 train set as well as all his books for paper salvage, so he arrived at married life with nothing but what he stood up in, as it were.

We all became experts in ingenuity, especially as far as clothes were concerned. Everything was purchased with coupons, so many for a yard of cotton, so many for a dress or skirt and two, I remember, for a man's handkerchief, which were in those days about the size of a squash court, and I made a very good shirt out of two silk ones, thus saving about eight coupons. Owing to the kindness of friends who contributed coupons, I did have a wedding dress, and a new suit to wear on our four-day honeymoon, which was all the leave Tony had. I also had a real, if minimal, trousseau. And a very real traditional wedding, with a cake made out of tinned butter from friends in America, fruit brought home by soldier brothers from the Middle East, and long-hoarded flour and sugar. Fortunately few people had sugar in their tea or coffee in our family. The families who did were in trouble when it came to weddings, and often had to have a false cover for the cake made of white cardboard with plaster squiggles on it.

No sooner were shops alive again and thriving than along came supermarkets, distorting the whole familiar retail map. I can't be objective about them because a) I really rather enjoy our local out-of-town one, which is of excellent quality, efficient and polite, and b) because I am not at all reliant on them, living in a village where I can buy almost all necessities, and where the shops, and shop assistants, fulfil their time-honoured rôle of also being social centres, an exchange for gossip or news, and the source of much personal kindness and consideration.

So my excursions to the supermarket are only engendered by the need for some out-of-the-way ingredient, or fish, or as an antidote to a culinary rut. I can therefore be completely anonymous and invisible, if I am in a hurry and have to complete my list as quickly as possible – though, even in haste, I can enjoy the colour and order of the carefully designed displays, or, if I have more time, I can enjoy my fellow shoppers, a rich source of entertainment. The admirable Richard Hoggart, in his book which is a social survey of his town, Farnham, describes how he uses supermarket shopping to size up people. Observing what they pile on to their trolleys he guesses just what sort of man or woman buys that selection of goods and lurks near them at the check-out to hear the voice and see if he is right.

I only ever entered that supermarket now and then *en route*, but since reading the book (which I enjoyed immensely) have given it a wide berth, divided between hoping my voice would match my trolleyfull and hoping it wouldn't, and in any case, nervous of Richard Hoggart's possible beady presence.

A few days ago, when all my shopping was done and I had been rewarded with a good helping of supermarket 'Street Theatre' (the elderly couple, shopping together, who couldn't agree on one single item – it took them about half an hour to get past the fruit and veg. The admirable girl who was so calm and patient when her two-year-old had the mother and father of all tantrums for at least ten ear-splitting minutes. The two cautious ladies who dithered and havered over every detail and took hours over it, ending at the check-out with two small pies and a packet of detergent and six eggs in a giant trolley), I had a bonus.

At the next check-out was a nice-looking young woman with two little boys aged about six and four. They were the most beautiful children I have ever seen in my life. It was a delight simply to look at them. Had they not been lively, merry, ordinary little boys they would have been too good to be true, and certainly no photograph or portrait would do justice to them. I lurked around them, putting more and more change into the charity box as an excuse for lingering, just enjoying them. I wondered if their mother knew how exceptionally beautiful they both were. Though clearly brothers, with the same thick fair hair and beautifully shaped blue eyes, they had very different faces, but equally lovely. It was dreadful to think of that peachy skin meeting its first shaver in years to come . . . However, they made my day.

For our daughters of course, shops have always been there, always full of stock, just as it was for their great-grandmother. Both are excellent cooks and both, when in the supermarket, need a pantechnicon rather than a trolley to take home the supplies to keep their families going.

Both are prudent shoppers, but our elder daughter gets carried away now and then. She left her laden trolley for a moment one day when she sought something else, and came back to find a man helping himself to the contents. Since everything in her trolley was labelled '20 pence off' or 'Buy two and get one free' or 'This week's Best Buy' he had thought it was a loss-leader bargain trolley and was busy taking advantage of it.

Obviously I also shop in towns, including London, and obviously now and then meet the sort of shop assistant who makes shopping a trial. Not often, but now and then. When it happens all one has to do is lie back and think of Glasgow. There – and it must be an inherited talent because it has always been so – there are real people behind the counter and what is more, they clearly regard you, the customer, as a real person too. It's a good start, no matter what, but even better that he or she seems really concerned that you can find what you want, as he or she always does.

On all my recent visits to Glasgow I have set out to seek this or that with trepidation, afraid that these people are no longer there, but they are. They make buying the dullest object a pleasure. They are morale-savers of the first order. So to anyone tempted only to shop via the Internet for ever more, I would suggest one last try, one last fling, but do it in Glasgow.

A Painting Wife

In the far-off days when Tony and I were first married wives accepted the fact that they had to live wherever their husband's work took them, and that was that. Even if wives worked outside the home (which was by no means the norm) this was a subsidiary activity and must be abandoned when the husband's job dictated a move.

I was lucky in being a painter, so I could continue to study and, with luck, acquire commissions wherever we were, though I had to wait until our last child had gone off to university, and we moved house and had enough room at last, to have my own studio. It is small. It is chaos. I paint nearer and nearer the door and then out into the passage as the rest of the room becomes silted up with a tide of paper and canvas and paints and boxes and bottles and jars for still life. Overhead masses of frames hang from my father's erstwhile saddle-racks, and not a single one of them is ever any good, in size or appearance, for whatever I am painting. One day I must have a frame bonfire. Meanwhile the studio is a blessed place where I can leave paints and palettes around. It has a north light, and when someone comes to have a portrait painted I devote several hours to clearing a path for the sitter, and always resolve to keep it that way, even while muttering to myself 'Dream on'.

As we moved around the country when the children were young I had to do a bit of adapting as at that time I was painting only in oils, and oils and small children are an uneasy mixture. I painted in whatever room I could, clearing away at the end of the day, and I could do this happily with a small Joanna. She was well satisfied with whatever was at hand, reshaping it or enhancing it to suit her desires, and she was not at all interested in eating my poisonous paints, or bashing things against a wet canvas.

Why I expected Andrew to behave like this is beyond me. He was a different person and a boy and not at all inclined to make his own world inside whatever confined him, such as being too young to walk, too small to reach, or confined within a cot, or in the parameters of good behaviour.

We have a giant drop-size cot. None of our children, grand-children, or junior visitors have been able to get out of it in babyhood, but Andrew could. All have slept there in peace and contentment. Andrew didn't. Thriving, highly coloured, gregarious and forthcoming, he couldn't be bothered with night-time for two interminable years. Tony and I took it in turns, and were soon able to sleep through each other's nights on duty. We moved him into Joanna's room (not as cruel as it sounds as she has inherited her father's gift for sleep) and he was slightly better, but still had a whole lot of ideas and conversation he wanted to convey at 3 a.m. So in the day we did all we could to tire him out but it was an uphill task. Any question of my doing some painting with Andrew secure in a nearby play-pen with lots of lovely toys was demonstrably absurd. In fact, paints lying anywhere in the house with the ever-exploratory crawling dynamo, were obviously a risk. It was not that there was any spare time in which to paint, rather that not being able to at all, even if I had time, nagged at me like toothache as I waited for the mythical opportunity.

There came a day when I had an idea that I *longed* to paint, and longed with such intensity that I no longer saw the stack of waiting ironing, the hoovering, the cooking and the sewing reproaching me inside the house, and the overnight weeds waiting for me outside in the garden. Tony was at the office, Joanna was at school; Andrew, aged one, and I were alone and I gazed at him thoughtfully while he gazed cheerfully back, and we both knew his play-pen full of fascinating, well-designed, toys, was not the answer. He wanted space and adventure and challenge. I wanted such a small space, but safe from him . . . why did it take me so long to see the solution?

I threw all the toys out of the play-pen, climbed in with my easel and paints, and let Andrew have the house. He was delighted by this. There I was, penned in out of his way and absorbed in my unfathomable activity, and he had all this wonderful freedom. He shot off and I could hear him scrambling about the house, talking to

himself, and he reappeared now and then with some treasure he had found to show me. (Once it was one of Tony's gold cuff-links, fallen behind the chest of drawers. I was deeply grateful that Andrew had brought it to me and not eaten it.)

The only time he got into serious trouble I was alert and there in a flash. He had found out how to unlock the glass cupboard, and was sitting in the middle of a sea of broken glass, delicately picking up strands in his fingers to show me. He was in fact un-scathed and tri-umphant, at the expense of a couple of dozen wedding present wine glasses. I never knew how he could have been so quick as I had leaped from the play-pen at the first sound of breaking glass.

Otherwise we spent many mutually satisfying winter mornings and his busy, busy, hours did make him sleep a bit better, if only a little, and this *modus vivendi* lasted until he found out how to walk. Then I had to think of something else. That was putting all my paints on to a big tray, and parking it, at the end of the day, on top of a high kitchen cupboard, where Andrew looked at it longingly but even he couldn't work out how to reach it.

The painting itself, on the easel, had to take its chance but was usually safe as he was not wicked, just curious, and he did his best not to touch it. It was only a mistake the day he tried to climb up the easel when I was out of the room, and the wet painting fell face down on the carpet via his thick, curly, blond hair. There were no magic cleaners in those days. Turpentine was my only solution. The carpet never recovered properly and after much turpentining and several shampoos Andrew's hair lost its pastel-tinted locks and streaks. I learned slowly about Andrew-proofing. Joanna had never been a hazard. For a start, she had never crawled and was seventeen months old before she rose to her feet and walked, having talked sensibly for some time before that. Anyway she was a girl – she knew what I was on about.

We had two children, five years apart, and I was deeply grateful and appreciative, having acquired them with some difficulty, and I was haunted by the ingratitude of my feelings when I felt that two children were not, properly, a family. I'd been one of four and Tony was one of six, and I couldn't see that two were more than a couple of children, however lovely as indeed ours were. However, I believed all the doctors who said I would not and could not find myself pregnant again, and really *did* know how lucky we were to have Joanna and Andrew.

Our GP at that time – an amiable Irishman who fished handfuls of the newly invented penicillin out of his trouser pocket and said 'Try her with some of these' when Joanna was feverish – refused to believe me when I said I was. I was insistent because I wanted the banana. Bananas had just, and fitfully, reappeared in some places, and anyone under five was entitled to one, and also pregnant ladies with a note to say so from the doctor. I saw this, in our case, as a banana for each child. There were pregnancy tests available in those dim dark, far-away days (though not, of course, for home use as now) but our Irish doctor only laughed at this idea, and said I was being hysterical.

Me? What time or chance did I have to be hysterical? Besides, I knew very well what pregnancy felt like. I had been there five times already, and I knew very well I was pregnant, possible or not. Finally, to shut me up ('Oh all right, you can have it this time but you won't be asking me in a month's time') I got my banana. Or rather Joanna got my banana, and Andrew had his own, and six months later we all had Tory, which was a good deal better for all of us than any amount of bananas.

Tory's arrival put everything into balance. There is great merit, from both the parental and children's points of view, to be able to say 'all the children' rather than 'both the children', and in being able to see compatible links through 'all the children'. Four or five or six children would no doubt be even better, but maybe not. I couldn't risk changing one iota of our highly individual offspring.

As for painting, and once free of play-pens, I could paint wherever I could find a corner, wherever we lived. Most places we lived in had an art school which I could attend in the evenings. Time was and is another matter but that is endemic. I *should* have more time now. I do, of course, have more time now, but where does it go? The urgency of my desire to paint still nags and, full of missionary zeal, and convinced that there are many people out there who could paint if only they had the courage to try, I do all I can to encourage them towards this delight. Only because I derive so much pleasure from painting (though also, I need hardly say, gloom and despair when it won't come right) and it seems to me such a peaceful occupation, taking up little space, making no noise, bothering nobody else, I was disappointed when none of our children would even try their hand.

One can't complain. They all found their own excellent and fulfilling routes and knew exactly what they were doing in their various ways, but I would have enjoyed their joy, had they found it in this hard and enchanting area. And all that was required, after all, was a little patience. We have now, among our grandchildren, three grandsons who are serious painters, and I have just had a happy half-hour on the telephone when one of them rang to discuss his painting plans and kit for his gap year. I think we could both have gone on about it for most of the afternoon.

A Holiday in France

In 1955 we used up our small and hard-won 'Rainy Day Fund' and took the children to France. We had not deprived them of proper summer holidays, and had had one most years but so far always in this country, rich in variety, and rain, and uncertain weather. In 1955 we all needed a holiday very badly, so we wanted it to be special and restorative. We had had no holiday the year before and the one before that was long forgotten because Tory, then nearly two, had become suddenly, terribly ill. Our excellent GP summoned an ambulance, and only when we were on our way did I realize we were not going to our local hospital but to London, to St Thomas's. With the alarm wailing all the 30 miles it was a horrible enough experience and must have been appalling for Tory, in the already nightmare state of high fever and distorted sight.

There was such haste at the hospital, rushing her – so minute on the long trolley – through corridors and up lifts and through endless swing doors until we reached doors which were shut firmly in my face. 'Sorry, mother, not in here. We'll let you know.' It was unbelievable. I am glad to say hospitals are not like that nowadays. Indeed nor was St Thomas's then in many departments as I found out later. As ever, these matters often depend on one person, and in this case a ward sister, clearly overdue for retirement. I was left on a landing by some stairs. There was a bench, and a tall, grimy window, and I waited there, praying. Praying also that Dr Nancy had been able to get through to Tony's office and that he would come, and he did, racing up the stairs, white-faced and bewildered. No less bewildered when I told him what had happened. 'You mean she may be dying and we are left out here? I don't believe it.' He tried to go through the swing doors. He did go, but Sister threw him out with ferocity. 'This is a grave emergency. You *must not* interfere.'

So we sat on the bench, while doctors and nurses came in and out, always avoiding our pleading eyes, or ran up and down the stairs, their footsteps clattering on the hard surface. It was a long time by any standard, but seemed to us like months, before a tall, thin consultant came out and addressed us. He didn't really look at us either. He paused just long enough to say 'You the parents?' Yes, we were, 'Well I can't tell you whether she has polio or meningitis or something else, but it is very odd and she is very ill' and before we could make any response he clattered briskly on down the stairs.

It was another long time before we were allowed to see her and then only briefly. She was enclosed in a glass-walled room, all alone in a big cot, so that she could be observed without nurses having to put on mask and gown, as they did when they went in to her. And as I did when I came to see her, which I was allowed to do for only half an hour a day.

As nobody could discover what was wrong they had to assume it was infectious. That meant Joanna and Andrew were not allowed to go to school and were in quarantine, so it was a problem finding kind friends who would look after them when I went to St Thomas's, by car, train and underground, and was away for the whole afternoon (all for the precious half-hour), as most of our friends had young children of their own.

Not one second over the half-hour were we allowed. Sister saw to that. Poor Tory had lumbar punctures and every kind of test and trial and paediatricians came from all over the place to see her. Once Tony's turn to visit coincided with one of these, and so he had to wait outside until the consultant had finished his examination. It took half an hour. When Tony then tried to enter Tory's room Sister was there, 'It's half-past four. No more visiting for today.' It seems ridiculous, now, that we put up with such treatment, and so added to Tory's considerable suffering by our absence. But it was not unusual hospital treatment in those days, and we were young and totally inexperienced about hospitals of any kind.

It was a long time before anybody could make reassuring sounds to us, but Dr Nancy was brilliant. Every day she rang to ask me what horror stories I had heard that day (given a disaster, so many people seek to soothe with tales of a worse one) and also to translate what she could learn of Tory's progress. And she did progress and at long last, recover, and Dr Nancy decided she was well enough to come home. St Thomas's refused, they said there were still paediatricians on their way to examine her, one from Italy and one – heaven help us – from China. Dr Nancy would have none of this, and one day she said 'Come on. We're going to London to fetch Tory.' Once there she told me to wait on the horribly familiar landing 'I can deal with Sister but I don't want to embarrass you, and there's a bit of paperwork to do.' I did hear her voice through the closed swing-doors. 'Nonsense, Sister. This is a child not a guinea-pig. I am taking her home' and so she did. We were prepared for Tory to be difficult and wary after such dreadful experiences and for so long, but she seemed to slide back into ordinary life exactly as before. I asked her what she would like as a special present, and she said at once that she would like a pastry hat, 'A what?' I said stupidly. She said 'You *know*. A pastry hat with flowers all round it. A pastry hat with lots of flowers.' Of course. A straw hat. Why didn't I recognize it at once?

She looked very delicious in it and wore it all summer, in the garden, fetching the others from school, and going to church, and it gave her and all of us great pleasure. Her calm return to ordinary life did not, unsurprisingly, last, and about six months later she began to dream ambulances and pain and fear, and would cling to me in terror if she heard a siren. In fact she clung to me all the time and was not happy if we were parted. So we weren't, for a year. Everywhere I went she went, to the dentist, to have my hair cut, to the osteopath, out to dinner (we could only accept dinner invitations if our hosts didn't mind Tory asleep in one of their beds or on a nearby sofa) and she was never a nuisance or obtrusive, asking only to be with us, and who can wonder? I knew that this phase would pass if she could work it out in her own way, and she did, emerging from it completely, and as healed as anyone could be after such a traumatic ordeal. So we were all in need of a good holiday, and as the 'Rainy Day Fund' would not take us far, we picked a village near Calais, called Equihen. It looked small, with plenty of beach and there was a modest family hotel there, so we booked in and set off, full of excited anticipation, taking the car on the ferry. Tory was by then three and a half, Andrew five and Joanna eleven, and we were a tight fit in our modest car, but were used to that and nobody moaned about it.

Equihen had had to begin all over again after the war. They had had to rebuild everything, once the ruins were cleared away, the streets and houses and church and school and mairie. By 1955 they had not done badly, and many of the inhabitants who had been evacuated to the Marne came back. Not all, of course. Some never came back. Some had never even reached the comparative safety of the Marne, and none returned to the known cottage, the familiar village, for it had all gone.

Instead the new village straggled upwards towards La Falaise, raw little concrete cottages interspersed with some blackened ruin nobody had bothered to remove. They had a school now, a long hut with a corrugated iron roof, behind the temporary church, and the mairie was another temporary building – a little concrete cube with two windows and a door, like a child's drawing, set on a square of pavement.

There were roads of a sort, and space for pavements, but the construction of these clearly came low on the list and mostly they were broad paths of rubble and pot-holes and no-colour dust. Only when one stood on the Falaise above them did the colour of the roofs relieve the monotone with dark orange or rusty brown. It was then that the contrast between the raw, half-finished village, exhausted by its own efforts, and the August fields around it showed most vividly. The stacked corn, precise and solid and shining gold in the sun, made a prim and satisfying pattern. The beet fields were jade green, and the uncut cornfields rippled as the breeze swept their tawny surface. And high in the summer sky, the larks sang over the cornfields and the ruins and the dusty new village, and endless stretches of sand and sea.

It was all we hoped for. All we wanted. The gimcrack village and the ruins and the concrete defence blocks still on the sand didn't matter a hoot. We had the sea and the sun and the larks overhead, and in the highest of spirits we drew up outside our little hotel. It was an excellent place. About a dozen families, all French except us, were staying there, and were so tightly packed into the dining-room that conversation could hardly be other than communal.

Before dinner, however, we had had time to rush down to the beach and take some photographs to prove this amazing event. *Us* in *France*! Travel (which meant crossing the Channel) was not taken for granted by one and all in 1955. And, here in exotic France, the sun shone just as it was supposed to do, and the photographs we took in that first hour show the girls laughing and skipping about on the beach. Not Andrew, however. Uncharacteristically, he is sitting on the sand, doing nothing, looking sad. He said he was tired and he looked it. He hung about, not interested, when further along the beach we came on the mussel gatherers among the rocks, and trudging up the steep cliff paths with heavy sacks over their shoulders.

Women with their black skirts pinned up to give freedom to their black-stockinged legs and heavy boots, their heads so firmly tied in scarves and set so stiffly on their shoulders that they seemed all one bent, burdened, piece. Young girls in coloured scarves and dirty dresses learned early to carry their sacks in the same slow, overburdened way. Boys in faded blue shirts walked like old men, and the old men walked doggedly. One by one, in twos and threes, they wound slowly up the cliffs from the sea. Andrew was glad when we had had our fill of the mussel gatherers, and turned back to the little hotel.

He wasn't hungry, he said, at dinner, though he tried to have some soup. Our friendly fellow-diners teased him amiably 'And you are tired? A big boy like you? Look at your little sister. She isn't tired by a little journey' and children edged through the chairs to talk to him. We were interesting because we were English, and our three matching bright-cheeked, fair-haired children attracted attention in any case wherever we went. Andrew was reluctant to leave the dining-room. 'It looks so feeble' he said testily but was clearly glad to be in bed, where I deposited him safely before returning to finish dinner. I wasn't more than twenty minutes but by the time I returned to him he had a high fever. This was from a standing start as in those days no mother travelled without a thermometer, which was whipped out at the slightest sign of trouble, and his temperature had been normal before dinner.

He had no rash or odd pains, but his temperature went up and up and up and within a couple of hours we needed a doctor. Tony tried to telephone but couldn't get through. 'It is cheaper and quicker' said Madame laconically 'to go and fetch him. It is only a twenty-minute drive.' When the doctor came he was reassuring. 'It is only la rougeole' he said. 'He'll have his rash by morning and in a week he'll be well enough to go home, though you must of course keep him in bed when you get there. Your own doctor will advise.' Tony and I looked at each other in mutual despair over poor Andrew's restless, burning form. There went our holiday. There went the summer altogether, as the girls hadn't had measles either.

A more immediate problem was presented by all our fellow guests. Andrew must have distributed measles lavishly around the dining-room. I hadn't appreciated how different was the French attitude towards infection from the English. At home, in the fifties, people, and most of all schools, were fanatical about quarantine. We'd had polio jabs and whooping cough jabs (though our children collected whooping cough in the surgery waiting-room when they went for their innoculation) but if measles jabs were invented then they hadn't come our way. Dr Nancy was ultra careful, and if she didn't trust them she would wait till they were trustworthy before advising her patients. In the morning, at breakfast, full of dread, I began to go round the dining-room and explain to all the families what we had inadvertently introduced. One and all responded gaily on the lines of

'Oh tant pis! Everyone must have la rougeole! No matter, no matter! If Etienne gets it, it will be good to have it over.'

No patient was ever nursed on an odder diet. When he began to want food again, he scoffed at the idea of the nursery food I thought proper for people in bed. He asked what we had had at lunch or dinner and selected the most exotic from our varied and unfamiliar menu. They were curiously remote and dreamlike, those hot days passed in his little gabled room, looking out over a bit of road and a bit of garden and the corner of the graveyard, and eating sea-food and aubergines and wild mushrooms with garlic with the reviving Andrew. All the strange food we never met at home he loved, and he has gone on in the same strain, a pleasure to cook for.

He couldn't see out of the window from his bed, so I would relate any event, and the smallest thing loomed large in such limbo surroundings. Such as a woman in a long, black skirt, hurrying along the road, pulling a child in a pink dress by the hand. As they reached the top of the rise a priest in a green-black cassock, his bare feet greenish in his sandals and riding a bicycle passed them, shouting and waving to them as he vanished over the hill. ('Have you noticed', said Andrew as I reported this, 'how different the French bicycles are from the English ones?' No, I hadn't, and as he detailed the various differences I marvelled that he had had the time or energy to observe all this.) The woman hurried on and the child, trotting beside her, began to cry. She stopped and lifted the child on to her back and strode on, the child hanging round her neck, the pink dress flapping up and down, showing small buttocks and thin legs gripping the black waist.

A sudden shower descended on a group of people dressed in their best one day when there was a wedding and they were *en route* for the church, all on foot so that was fun. And on another day there was a funeral, and all the mourners very, very old (so presumably returners from the Marne) made a sad, slow, black snake all along the road.

We had books, of course (never moving without plenty of those) and we made up puzzles and played 'Beggar-My-Neighbour' and 'Clock Patience', and outside the heat shimmered, and down on the beach Tony and the girls were doing what one does on a lovely empty beach, swimming, drying in the sun, and reading. The problem was that both Tony and Joanna were reading *Le Rouge et Le Noir*, and there was a good deal of mild wrangling over it. Each said the other was the usurper but before long Joanna was able to give in gracefully and let him have it all to himself because she read much more quickly than he did and had soon finished. Tory needed no further diversion than the beach itself. She made sand castles and collected shells and scrambled about the rocks, self-contained as ever. I had turns of the beach, of course, while Tony mounted guard, and when the strange week had passed we set out for home, spending the very last of the 'Rainy Day Fund' on a cabin on the ferry so that we wouldn't spread measles through the whole ship.

Entering our extremely nice kitchen again, after one week instead of the long-anticipated two I *loathed* it. If I had had a sledge hammer handy I would have smashed the cooker. It was not as though we could go away again, or drive down to the nearest sea, crowded as it would be, because Joanna and Tory had yet to have their measles. We all did all we could to encourage it. They drank Andrew's left-over lemonade, finished his uneaten food, and they were all together non-stop, head to head, reading and drawing and playing games.

It was just as well they seemed to be having quite a happy time with each other as they were all still pariah dogs, as it were, and we could have no visitors unless they were brave enough to ignore the quarantine and few were. Tory duly acquired her measles, but Joanna refused it. She has had plenty of chances of acquiring measles since, and has always refused it. Talk about anti-climax . . .

Return Visit

It was time, I felt, when Tory was three, Andrew five and Joanna ten, to take these poor little Sassenachs to visit Glasgow.

Not, alas, back to Clairmont Gardens, the house having been requisitioned during the war, and after that being converted to offices, so Granny was living near the university, in Oakfield Avenue. With her was her dear friend and companion, Edith, who had first come to her as personal maid long before I was born, and stayed until Granny's death, nursing her through her long last illness with devotion and flashes of her own black humour.

A few doors away Aunt Nan was living in the house originally bought for Grandad's parents, and since then lived in by the two bachelor uncles, his brothers. When the brothers died and Aunt Nan inherited it she had no need to acquire furniture or pictures or beautiful china or glass. Having never in all her long life had her own home she had never assembled such things, and now she just moved quietly into the uncles' house, among all their familiar and fascinating possessions, and continued the life she had always led.

It was a relief to find such a Clairmont Gardens atmosphere in the little Oakfield Avenue house. Partly because of the lighting from a sky-light over the stair-well, which echoed the great cupola over the long, green stairs in the former house. Joanna found this lighting peculiar, but all the same a relief in what she remembers as a dark house in a dark city, although the darkness was only physical and it remains in her mind as a place of pleasures. All the buildings were either dark grey or heavily shaded with dark grey, and in the cleanest of houses soot would form a gritty surface on everything as soon as a window was opened a mere crack.

Apart from the light on the stairs, much of the Clairmont Gardens atmosphere obtained. Familiar pictures and looking-glasses and ornaments were around, and the same comfortless drawing-room

139

chairs, and the same sag-bellied Crown Derby coffee cups and the same caper with the Cona coffee machine after dinner. The matching Crown Derby tea cups, which were so lovely to drink tea from because they were as thin as paper had, to Granny's frequently lamented sorrow, been pinched, with much else, during the years her furniture was in storage. And, of course, there was the deliciously familiar warm welcome for all of us, arriving late and tired and thrilled to be back.

Tony, having lived and worked in Glasgow, fully shared my feelings for the city and its people, and so the wary children had had two parents, rather than one, telling them what a wonderful place it was.

On our first morning Tony was required to take Aunt Nan to some appointment or other, so I took the children to Sauchiehall Street to see if Lyon's toy shop was still there. It was during the last days of the trams, and we were near the university terminus. As we walked there Tory, the three-year-old, asked 'What is that *disgusting* smell?' I, loyal and unthinking, said 'That's not a disgusting smell. That's the Kelvin.' Even as I spoke, hearing my own words, I realized what a disgusting smell it was, a thick, slightly sweet, brown, all-pervasive smell. Tory was not convinced by my answer, and held her nose with her rain-wet fingers until we were inside the waiting tram. (I am happy to say that, on a recent visit, I can report an utterly smell-free Kelvin.)

The tram was by no means ready to go. The conductor sat contentedly on a front seat reading a newspaper and, through the glass, the driver did the same. Rain poured down outside, running down the windows in streaks, distorting our view of umbrellas hurrying by. Three pairs of eyes were fixed on me expectantly, wondering when the glories of Glasgow were about to start. Tory said she was glad to be out of the smell. Andrew gazed dreamily into the middle-distance whenever his large, mild, eyes left my face and I knew what he was dreaming about. Oakfield Avenue had one major advantage over Clairmont Gardens, in the shape of a bronze, turbaned figure of an African child in the place of the newel-post at the foot of the stairs, and he had fallen in love with her. He was always tactile and she felt wonderful and he parted from her with reluctance. At long last the driver moved, the conductor looked at his watch and folded his newspaper into his jacket pocket, and picked up his ticket machine. We were the only passengers, so he came up the car in a leisurely way and stood looking at us. He smiled at Joanna and Andrew, but he said to Tory 'Would ye like to clip yer own ticket, hen?' 'It's all right,' I thought. 'We're home.'

We did all the proper things, treading in maternal and grand-maternal footsteps. We went to gaze at Clairmont Gardens, and found it and all the graceful surrounding terraces smothered with the cars of the office workers who were now using all or parts of the houses. We went to the Art Gallery, which they loved as much as we had always done, and there we could, as ever, examine the exquisite model yachts, including Sir Thomas Lipton's *Shamrock*, which had won the America Cup.

Family legend always said that Grandad's cutter, the *Annasona*, which he acquired in 1880 and which became famous on the Clyde for all the prizes she won, among them the Queen's Cup at Cowes, could have given *Shamrock* a fitting challenge in the America Cup, only Grandad had other and better things to do with his money. Just as we had done as children, we went from the model yachts to see the vast, glittering, silver trophies *Shamrock* had won, and gazed at them awestricken. Our children could not, of course, compare them with the array of similar trophies in the Clairmont Gardens dining-room that we had known so well, and which were now dispersed. It had always made us feel complacent to look at all the Lipton silver and know that not one was as lovely as Grandad's silver castle, with every stone depicted and every door and window perfect, and a tiny silver portcullis. It seemed a desecration when anyone lifted the roof off to help themselves to a biscuit.

I am glad that our children saw the Lipton silver then, for they couldn't now. It is still there but so tarnished that it looks as if it is made of crumpled brown paper. In all the neglect and deterioration throughout that magnificent gallery, once a fitting example of, and tribute to, the energy and industry of Glasgow, the silver, in the Lipton cases and elsewhere, was the worst. I have never seen such ill-kept silver on public display except in the Silver Museum in Lima, where it was all like that. But Lima is not a city famous for order or prosperity, so it wasn't so surprising there.

In the picture galleries I found all my favourites for the children's delight. Joanna was properly enslaved by Rembrandt's 'Man in Armour' and they all enjoyed the Colourists and quite right too, in my prejudiced view.

The Kelvingrove Park hadn't changed one iota, and we duly fed the ducks and then went up the hill to visit Lord Roberts. There he was, dear fellow, competing as ever with his horse to see which of them could look most noble, and between them an uplifting sight.

We went to the Botanic Gardens and then to the Cathedral, to inspect the window their great-grandfather had given, and in which their grandmother (whom they knew as Mia) is depicted as an angel.

And we went to tea at Park Terrace, where the widowed Aunt Gaickie still lived. Joanna remembers well the cosy, loving, warmth of her welcome and the traditional Park Terrace tea, with delicious triangular chocolate biscuits and shiny brown cookies. And the nursery, where in the cupboard there were still long-forgotten toys and games, which the three children happily played with . . . but I was glad to escape the nursery when it was time to go home, so shrouded in dust-sheets and empty and abandoned it seemed. It was, however, several floors above kind, loving Aunt Gaickie and the warm fire and the silver teapot, and Uncle Bertie's wonderful painting of the sea in the hall. She seemed so unchanged and I am glad to remember her so, for it was the last time I kissed her goodbye at the top of the steps. Soon afterwards the house was given to the university and Aunt Gaickie went to live with Aunt Nan, and the two devoted sisters spent their last years together, and in death were only separated by a few months.

All our children have returned to Glasgow since they grew up, for a few days' recreation, or *en route*, or whatever, and always with pleasure.

Though Joanna is now there often, her next visit, after our stay in Oakfield Avenue when she was ten, was when she was grown-up, married, and with a two-year-old daughter, a little curly headed blonde so like she had been at that age that I became confused in the generations.

Tony and I, with Joanna and Louise, went north for the wedding, in Glasgow Cathedral, of my best friend's daughter, my godchild, another Rosemary. It was a splendid wedding and we were all very spoiled throughout, with every detail forethought and taken care of, so we couldn't fail to enjoy the whole visit. I am not sure, however, that Louise didn't enjoy most of all the long, dreary, tedious train journey. For her it wasn't tedious at all, but full of interest, and she was fully occupied in taking in everyone and everything around her. She was, as ever, full of conversation though she confined it to her family. Amiably and politely, she refused to flirt with the young man opposite who tried every trick he knew to make her talk to him. He was amazed and amused that someone so small could talk so well. Little he knew. In our family we were well used to it. Not a single baby among our children and grandchildren (though I have yet to see how great-grandchildren will turn out) has been slow to talk, and one or two have seldom stopped.

As we neared Glasgow, and Louise should have been tired out, she decided to give the persistent young man a treat after all. She got up on the table and danced, keeping her balance remarkably in the shoogly train, and she smiled at him at long last, even though she still wouldn't talk to him. A dance was all he was going to get. As the train slowed she sat down again. 'Well, that's done' she said. 'Now it's Glasgow.'

The See-saw

It would be a strange child who thought his or her parents had got it right. In their turn, striving not to repeat the mistakes of their own upbringing, they make others with their own children, trying to guide them and protect them and encourage them in their journey to adult status. Just as in earnestly trying to guard a toddler against danger, one can never foresee the totally unexpected, or bizarre, hazard which is lying in wait, so each generation makes new parental wrongs.

When our children were small, and we moved house, we found a splendid see-saw in the garden. The children and their friends all enjoyed it immensely and when, many years later, we moved again, we took the see-saw with us. It was only when I saw grandchildren playing with it that I realized its lethal qualities. In this house I have a good view of the see-saw from the kitchen window and have therefore witnessed horrific episodes, such as small children being boun- ced off the top end by much heavier brothers and flying through the air like shuttle-cocks, or wandering into the path of the lower end as it crashes to the ground, complete with flailing trainer-clad feet.

It is no wonder that all the grandmothers are reputed to be fusspots. Of course they are. They have

lived through it all before and have no desire to push their luck. In any case, young mothers are (and have to be) protected by youthful hope and ignorance, and thus enable their children to do their own exploring and find their own adventures and mis-adventures so that, with luck, they can grow up well adjusted and with enough confidence to take on the future. Grandmothers can remember having this laid-back attitude and it tends to give them the creeps.

It is, of course, all a matter of perspective. I see now that the training our son imposed on us in his early years had to be well absorbed so that, as grandparents, we could deal with his sons. (Our daughters, though they had the normal troubles and disasters, never put us through this particular mill.)

When Andrew was two, and it was a summer Sunday evening and he and Joanna were safely in bed, I went off to Evensong, leaving Tony gardening in the beds around the house so that he could be on guard. It was all very quiet and peaceful and the children were asleep, so he could concentrate on his weeding and pruning. Andrew, however, was not asleep. He climbed out of his cot and decided to sail boats in the bath. It was an enormous old-fashioned bath with huge taps, so it didn't matter that he couldn't reach to put the plug in: he soon had a splendid bathful. Then he had no need to confine himself to bath water, as his boats, and his bedroom slippers and several books sailed across the landing and down the stairs. He was entranced. In no time he could splash into his bedroom, ours, the spare room, Joanna's room, and the stairs resembled a water-fall.

At this point his busy father noticed what was happening and galloped upstairs to rescue the peacefully sleeping Joanna, who was at first startled and then terrified because, carrying her down the cascading stairs, he said 'I just hope the bloody ceiling is not going to come down' and she thought he meant the house was all going to collapse. I returned to find him desperately mopping up, a happy, soaked Andrew jumping about in the lake in the hall, and Joanna sobbing 'Don't go in there. Don't go in there. I *can't* stop Daddie and Andrew but the house is going to fall down.'

It was about a year later and I was cooking when Andrew appeared in the kitchen, bashed, bruised and covered in blood, though not tearful. '*Darling*,' I said, 'what on earth has happened to you?' 'I rode my bike off the edge of the terrace' he said cheerfully. 'It was a big crash' and he wiped the dripping blood out of his eyes. 'It's an 8 foot drop' I said, appalled. 'How could you do that?' 'I just wasn't looking. Shall I show you how I did it?' he said. It was an offer I declined . . .

Now and then I wondered if I would manage to live through his childhood, even if he did. All it did, of course, was to pile up the potential-hazard stack in my mind, waiting for grandchildren. But one learns that however high the stack, there is still something else. A generation later Andrew's sons, Harvey and Francis, were staying with us while their parents had a holiday, and it was a treat for us to have them. They never seemed at a loss for something to do, or bored, or quarrelsome, so we were all having a very pleasant time.

I went into an upstairs room one morning and was greeted by Harvey's voice – a distinctive voice, even at seven it was deep and rich. I looked around and couldn't see him and he spoke again and I saw to my absolute horror that he was outside the window. 'How did you get there?' I asked in a small and strangled tone. 'By the drainpipe' he said blithely. By the drainpipe . . .

The frail old drainpipe lightly attached to the even older and more fragile wall, and the hard surface of the court-yard below . . . I said 'If I open the window, can you reach to get in?' 'Not actually' he said. 'It's a bit far. I'll go back down.' He called down 'Go down again Francis', so that I realized there was not one but two stalwart boys on the drainpipe which couldn't have been guaranteed to support a sparrow. I couldn't bear to watch the descent, but pausing only to say 'Go back then, carefully. If Grandfather sees you he'll kill you' before flying downstairs with some vague notion of catching them as the guttering collapsed. Of course they landed safely, as they have often done before and since when I wasn't there to see, but we hadn't finished with that day.

Rain began, so they abandoned an exploration of the loft in the barn (where they found a wasps' nest, *fortunately* not in use) and came indoors. Climbing was clearly still pulsing through their veins, and their laughter and shouts led me to the stairwell, over which they were swinging. I considered stopping them, but they seemed so happy and sure-footed that I trusted to luck and left them to it. My trust was misplaced. Francis missed a foot-hold and fell, knocking himself out. He was only out for a minute but I'd had time to ring the doctor. A locum came, a competent-seeming man who examined him thoroughly and said he was sure he would be fine when he had slept off the shock 'but don't let him get drowsy'. 'How do I know' I asked 'the difference between being sleepy and being drowsy?' 'Oh you will,' said the departing doctor, 'mothers do.' I did hope earnestly that grandmothers also did, but luckily Francis didn't test me. He went to sleep at once and woke refreshed and bright-eyed and asking what was going to happen next.

I hardly liked to think. We decided, eventually, to go to Marwell Zoo, which would involve a good long walk to use up surplus energy, and fascinating birds and beasts to see all the way along. It was a sunny afternoon, and we watched lions and tigers – often very distant but all the same exciting – and informed ourselves about the different kinds of zebras, and spent ages watching the most diverting wallabies, with distracted and exasperated wallaby mothers trying to look after babies, while adolescents fooled around and showed off and teased their younger siblings. Eventually we came to a large sloping field labelled 'Cranes'. The cranes were all in the far corner of the field and very distant. Only three artificial cranes, made of lead or resin or some such, were near the railings as we clutched the bars, peering through and trying to make out what the distant cranes would be like if we could get near enough to find out. Suddenly one of the artificial cranes turned round and bit Francis sharply on his thumb. It was a very nasty surprise for us all, especially as the biter at once went back to being completely motionless, so that we could hardly have believed it had happened were it not for the evidence of Francis's bleeding thumb. He was very gallant about it, and for days afterwards proudly wore the badge I made for him, which said 'I have been bitten by a Stanley Crane'.

It is easy to see why perfect parenthood is beyond us all. Starting as apprentices, knowing nothing in most cases (certainly in mine) a whole new, if small, person is placed in your erratic care. Small, helpless, and barely articulate, but all the same a complete, formed person whose subsequent experiences will only modify, and never change, what is already there. It is awe-inspiring.

I read the other day of a university research programme which had concluded eventually that 'babies of two or three weeks could take in far more than had been previously supposed'. Supposed by whom? Not by me, or anyone else who has been lucky enough to bring up babies. We know very well that a new-born baby is taking it all in, and that therefore one must be careful what one says in front of him or her from the very first moment. They may not have learned the words but they know all about tone and atmosphere and what is in your mind, and you are a fool to forget it, even for a moment.

Nowadays, when small children are playing on our see-saw, I watch their parents with admiration as they sit relaxed and happy, drink in hand, letting the see-saw crash up and down in the back-ground. Exactly as I did once. Exactly as they have to do, to let their children find out for themselves. The see-saw has recently had a new plank, and will therefore go on for years and years yet, giving pleasure, being fun, being lethal, unless and until some EU legislation orders its destruction or decrees that nobody should play on it except in a suit of armour. That will be terrible. One more step towards the appalling day when the whole nation will be covered and smothered by a blanket woven out of shredded, justifiably anxious, grandmothers.